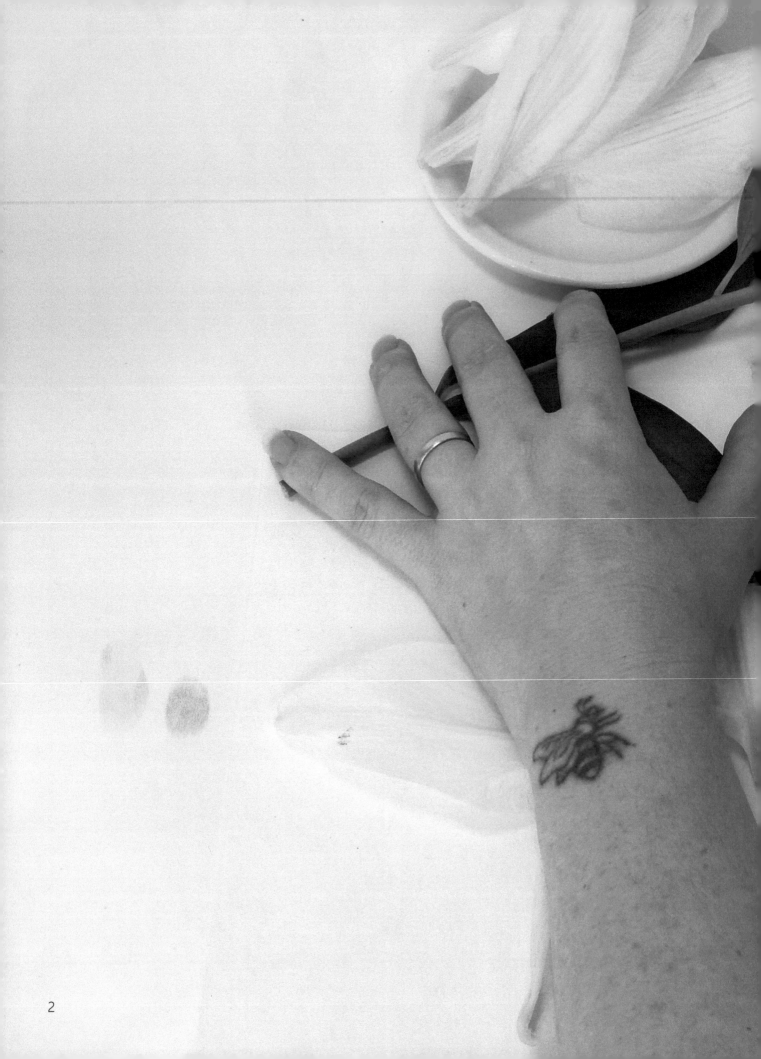

the effortless floral craftsman

— a floral crafter's guide to crafting with nature —

Christine de Beer

photographs by Christine de Beer

First published in 2018

Photographs by Christine de Beer
Photographs in this book (except for the cover) were cropped and placed for layout, but not altered.

www.christinedebeer.ca
christine@christinedebeer.ca
Copyright © Christine de Beer

ISBN: 978-1-9993923-2-1

contents

For Marius

who told me to trust my talent

introduction

Ef·fort·less

Adjective

achieved with admirable ease

The Effortless Floral Craftsman is a pictorial guide on becoming your own kind of effortless floral craftsman. The book is filled with how-tos and why-tos to inspire floral crafters, from beginners and designers with some experience who are collecting ideas, to advanced designers on the never ending journey to mastering their craft, whether you are crafting your work for passion or profit, or passion and profit.

Our floral journey begins with a look at how we develop our effortless style, at first emulating the work of masters and ultimately branching out to make our own unique contribution to the craft.

I unpack my tool bags and open up my design room to help you set up your own design space in which your talent may flourish. I simplify harvesting, purchasing, and conditioning plant material by teaching you how to look at these processes from the plant's perspective, and I demonstrate hydration techniques and how to support flowers in your designs.

By paging through the core techniques that I use to craft my work with, you can identify the skills and techniques that are part of your tool bag of creative resources you draw upon to craft your work, and add to this those you have not yet explored. I show how and why I test design rules, how and why studying nature helps us to create believable floral illusions and why knowing how and why can help us remain inspired to clearly interpret a unique floral story in our own effortless style. You will also notice that my creative processes touch on basic principles of creativity that you can use as inspiration for mastering other artistic pursuits, but this part I leave to you to unfurl.

Next I suggest a strategy for sharing creativity in a supportive and encouraging way, an approach that is fair to our own vision and expression, and to the creative flower community we are part of.

The book closes with an observation about confusing (yet enchanting) plant names and how to take the stress out of getting the pronunciations just right.

Christine de Beer

Let's design...

craftsmanship
of masters, apprentices ... and journeyman

For as long as we have been creative, we have recognized true skill and have strived to emulate it.

And for as long as we have strived to emulate skill, we have had masters who have taught by example and apprentices and journeymen who have learned by imitating and invigorating this example.

My own creative journey is, for the most part, the contemporary version of this old tradition. Like most, I learned first by imitating, and then grew from there. If we explore this traditional way of mastering a craft as a path for our own continuous creative journey, it quickly becomes clear how mutually beneficial it is for us to connect regardless of our level of expertise. With this in mind, I captured, wrote, designed, and chose the how-tos in this book. My intention is that this book will serve as a contemporary resource throughout our floral craftsmanship journey, whether you identify with being an experienced master, a novice apprentice, or a journeyman who is no longer an apprentice but has begun your own journey to become a new breed of master.

It is helpful to consider that labeling the stages of creative development was never intended to pigeonhole, grade, or limit the craftsman. The journeyman is in no way superior to the apprentice, and the apprentice in no way inferior to the master.

Instead they depend on each other to keep their craft vital and relevant. In fact, this symbiotic relationship between the master, apprentice, and the visiting journeyman preserves the craft form they have deemed so worthy of their time.

Part of the master's development is becoming secure enough in her own signature craft that she is comfortable with seeing her life's work being copied.

So secure that she can see it copied perfectly, stick by stick and petal by petal. But also so secure that she can let it go in such a way as to see that same work copied in someone else's perfectly... imperfect way.

This is the honour of being a master, and it is also the price of being a master.

Part of the apprentice's development is recognizing the skill of a particular master that will most resonate with one's own creative spark, and then patiently dedicating his time and effort to acquire the skills needed to understand and ultimately copy the work of the master, perfectly.

This is the honour being an apprentice, and it is also the price of being an apprentice.

There can be no master without an apprentice.

Without exposure to the fresh and enthusiastic world in which the apprentice is developing, the master is at risk of becoming stuck in a habitual way of creating, and of forgetting what attracted her to the craft in the first place. The apprentice is not experienced enough to know that something will "just not work," and the master is reminded that sometimes things "do just work." Under the eager, learning eyes of the apprentice, the master is reminded to be masterful. Without an apprentice, the master can easily forget the very fundamentals of the craft and become so self-involved and focused on the complexities of striving for perfection, that no real growth happens anymore. In time, the master's once-groundbreaking efforts become commonplace, habitual, familiar, and ultimately quite dull. The master becomes bored . . . and boring. An elitist approach causes us to lose touch with our craft and to foolishly dismiss a new contribution of value simply because it is "just not how we have always done it."

Without exposure to a master, the apprentice can easily convince himself that he is already good enough, never realizing how much there is still to learn and how great he could become.

The master and apprentice grow together, becoming better and stronger with every interaction. In time, the apprentice will be ready to contribute his unique spark to the craft, and the master will encourage him to head out to pursue a wider creative journey. The apprentice now becomes a journeyman.

The journeyman is a skilled craftsman who travels from master to master, collecting and sharing knowledge, cross-pollinating expertise. She has mastered the fundamentals of her craft and has moved on from merely copying the work of a master, to searching for new skills and mastering her own signature. The journeyman pushes boundaries by taking the craft beyond the limitations of the known, forever altering the craft with her distinct contribution. In other words, she is becoming a master.

This is the honour of being a journeyman, and it is also a form of compensation to the master who is exposed to "what is happening out there" and "what happened right here." The master can see the influence that her own life's work has had on the industry by witnessing that work expanded, explored, and renewed, in a brave and unencumbered way, through the hands of a skilled craftsman. Ideas are challenged, and growth happens for all.

It is invigorating to watch an apprentice, eager and wide-eyed with curiosity and enthusiasm. It is pure inspiration to see a journeyman who is not fazed by limitations, creating work that infuses others with newfound energy to create and master one's own craft. Ultimately, it is awe-inspiring to watch a true master seemingly effortlessly at work.

because | here is the simple truth about mastering a craft:

The more skilled you get, the less you will feel like you have mastered this at all. You will never again feel as accomplished as you did the first time you finished a design and thought: This looks pretty good, I think I should learn how to craft with nature...

Today, the lines between apprentice, journeyman, and master are somewhat blurred, but techniques and craftsmanship are still great sources of inspiration.

The lines between art and craft forms are also less defined, and it is not unusual to see influences from and find inspiration in all areas of our lives. I strongly believe in cross-pollinating skills, and I am a technique collector. Techniques usually capture my imagination long before an inspiration or idea for a design hits me.

Visit a thatcher, a cricket bat maker, a hedge layer, a broom squire, a weaver, and a local basket maker—if you can still find one. Of course, learning a craft also helps to preserve these skills. You do not have to be a master in every craft form you encounter on your creative journey. Just be open to the learning experience. Pick up what you find fascinating, then see if you can make it your own. I learned about natural dyes from a silk painter, was inspired to use wax as a waterproof barrier after watching a batik artist, and I learned how to buff flax from a rope maker.

Take a class. Be curious. Find the masters. Be inspired by the journeymen. Cheer on the apprentices. Make your art.

It is a rewarding and hugely personal journey to develop and ultimately master your own creative voice.

tools, equipment, and design space

"the way might just be a way and not at all your way."

Like a tender shoot grows through a crack in concrete, art finds a way to get itself made with or without tools, equipment, or the ideal space. You do not need so much stuff. But you might want some stuff so that, just like the skills and techniques you are discovering and mastering, you can use the resource when inspiration hits.

In this chapter I tell you about my two toolboxes, what is in them, and how I custom-make some tools and equipment. I also show you how I use these tools and equipment through a few design examples. Then I show you bits of my tiny design room, how I store my odds and ends so that my workspace is (almost . . . goals!) always design ready and picture-worthy.

In the previous chapter, I spoke of the masterful designer who makes creating brilliant designs look effortless. Did you imagine her trying to make do with the wrong glue or working on a wobbly table? Probably not. Nor should you.

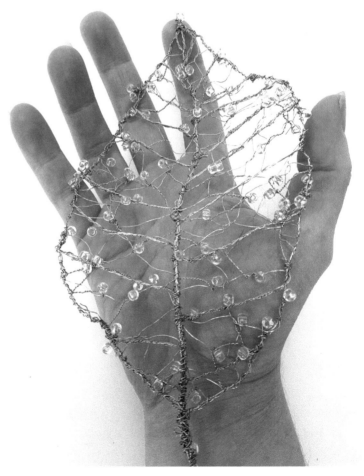

tool bags

Any craftsman will beam with happiness when you compliment her tool bag. It's our pride and joy! It often takes as long to build up our tool bag as it takes to acquire our skills.

I love asking my design neighbours at shows about their tool bags. There is always an interesting story attached, and the bag itself says a lot about the designer. Some designers carry many boxes, others only a carpenter's belt. Some have a box that doubles as a chair or stepladder, while others have carts on wheels.

The contents are just as fascinating. Look past the commercially available items, and you will find those trusted tools that were either handmade by the designer or modified in some way.

I have two tool bags filled with things that I either treasure, or that were custom-made to suit my design style. The one bag is larger and has plenty of cute compartments and pouches for my tiny bits and pieces that I use in my design room. Even though it is really pretty, it is bulky and heavy, so it is more of an easy-to-reach display container. My other bag, my take-along bag, is smaller and lighter and filled with portions of items, packed and repacked depending on the project. In both cases, I am a disciplined packer. There is simply no space for rusty, old, or unusable stuff. I travel extremely light!

The real value of a great tool bag cannot be measured in money. The worth lies in whether it suits the individual designer. Invest time and energy in stocking your tool bag. Pack only the equipment that works for you and represents what you stand for as a designer.

tools

Always reach for the right tool to get the job done efficiently.

When your problem is a stuck screw, a knife is not a screwdriver, it is a frustration. How long do you snip with blunt scissors at wildly fraying ribbon before your vocabulary becomes creative?

Visit your local hardware store and ask questions. Look at the tools you use every day in your design space and ask a craftsman that uses similar tools to teach you how he uses them, and why he uses them in that particular way.

It is amazing to see the difference in the ease of work and in the results when you really understand the tools you use. You cut straighter with a knife, and with less effort, when you use your shoulder muscles. Secateurs are easier to use when you employ your elbow. The secret of effortlessly using a saw is in your stance and in the position of your waist ... who knew!?! Once you have the know-how, you become comfortable with it ... or not. Either way, own it.

Are you proud of your tools?

I would advise that you buy the best you can possibly afford. "The best" is defined as those tools that work best for you. This really holds true for all things you use in your pursuit to master your craft. You are investing in your own development.

Every purchase, flower, or accessory should be cared for in a way that inspires respect, gratitude, and pride by the designer. In turn, that will inspire respect, gratitude, and pride in the onlooker, recipient, or client. Take care of your stuff and make it last.

It is part of a craftsman's design philosophy.

Spend a little bit of time at the end of the day to clean up. Wipe down your knife and treat it with oil. You have put in a great day's work, and tomorrow deserves a clean and inspiring start.

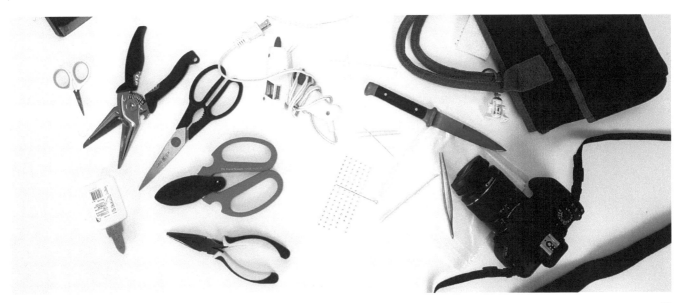

military knife

My knife is sharp, tough, rustproof, well balanced, and has a comfortable weight.

It's built to work hard and cut like a dream and is by far my favourite tool in my bag! I use it to cut flowers, whittle woody stems, pry things open, remove bark, and even cut candle wax.

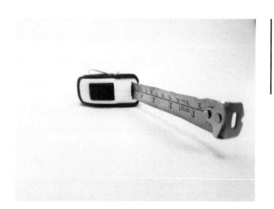

tape measure

Inches on the one side and centimeters on the other. No need to convert anything when you are at an international show.

pliers

You might need more than one pair, depending on your design style. Look for heavy-duty pliers that you don't have to be careful with, and a smaller pair that is used for jewelry making, for thin decorative wires.

drill

A battery-operated drill is really convenient. Always drill on a block of wood so that you don't accidentally damage your work surface.

tweezers

Tweezers are great for fine, delicate designing. Tweezers are also a helpful tool to remove bits that fall into tiny spaces or to position items in awkward gaps.

cuticle stick

I use these while weaving. The stick guides any blade of grass or delicate stem without bruising or causing damage.

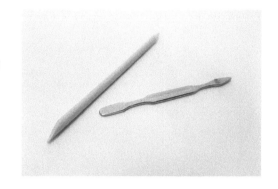

shower curtain or plastic lining

Shower curtains are great to work on as the plastic lining protects surfaces in your design room or on location. The plastic catches drips and plant material, making it fast and easy to clean up. Also, you can use the plastic sheets to line containers.

A large shower curtain or plastic sheet can also double as a backdrop for a few on-location pictures of your design.

butterfly clips

Clip out the inside pins, and you have the perfect little claws to keep stems in place while glue dries. Clips are also ideal to hold orchid stems to a support wire. Of course, this tool will also clip away that irritating strand of hair that keeps slipping into your eyes on a bad hair day.

I have sap green, natural green, and brown orchid clips for when I want to leave the clips in the design but have them be less visible. I also have bright pink, glittery butterfly clips for temporary use. The bright colour is a trick so that I don't forget to remove them.

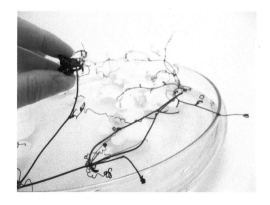

florist scissors

Florist scissors are sharp, precise, and easy to use. Keep your scissors clean by wiping them with a soapy wet cloth and treating them regularly with mineral oil.

heavy duty, all-purpose scissors

A pair of "would probably be able to cut anything" scissors really helps when constructing armatures.

ribbon scissors

And then I keep a pair of "nothing but ribbon" scissors, making sure they are as sharp as possible.

tiny precision scissors

You will be surprised how often you need to snip out something tiny to keep your designs well groomed. These are perfect. Look for them in a manicure kit, or you can use embroidery scissors.

cable ties

Great to secure things fast. You can get cable ties in almost any colour.

water mister

Orchids love a water mist. Roses not so much. Different types of plant material will respond differently.

Do not mist any item constructed from wood glue techniques because water weakens the glue. Never mist anyone's design but your own, especially if you are not sure what magic they used to keep it all together.

tape

Stock florist tape for wired flowers. Painter's tape is useful for temporarily taping things together but then removing them without ripping into the surface. Use clear tape to make an invisible grid over the top of a vase to keep flowers in place.

Use double-sided tape to glue leaves to the side of a vase.

Keep a marker with your tape. You never know when you will need a black mark. It's also helpful to temporarily mark your vases or supplies when you pool resources with other designers. Cut a small strip of tape that can be written on and later be easily removed from a surface, stick it on the item (somewhere it won't be seen), and write your name on it. It really cuts down on confusion when you are in a hurry to vacate a competition hall and have no time to figure out what goes where.

Masking tape is also a fantastic placeholder. You can stick it on the floor or work area to make sure you are within the space you are allocated.

pins in foam

I keep my pins stuck in foam. This way, pins won't get stuck in me when I rummage through my bag to find something, nor will they spill out of a box at the worst possible moment.

By pulling out the pins slightly, you can use the pin heads as a drying rack for beads or tiny flowers, keeping them safe while the glue dries.

how-to | pin a flax roll

Roll flax strips tightly.

Press a pin through the flax to secure.

glue

hot glue

Every glue gun should be sold in kit form: gun, dinner plate, and a bowl for ice water. The ice water is for an emergency to immediately cool down a burn, and the plate is to rest under your gun to catch stray drops.

hot glue pan

Great for dipping items to be glued.

how-to | remove hot glue strands

When you glue a structure with hot glue, inevitably a few stray strands of glue will become stuck all over the design.

Melt the unwanted strands away with a hairdryer.

Set the hairdryer on the highest (warmest) setting. Because the strands are so thin, they don't need a lot of heat to simply melt away. Do not focus the heat on any section long enough to melt the glue connection. Simply heat until the strands start to melt.

how-to | spin hot glue strands

Deliberately spin hot glue strands for web designs.

Press out a good amount of glue onto two pieces of Styrofoam.

Press the two pieces together and slowly pull apart to create long glue strands.

Wrap the glue strands over your design for a natural-looking web.

To create raindrops, spray the glue web with water.

how-to | glue a radial baby's breath stem armature

The easiest way to craft a radiating stem design is to cut, position, and glue the stems in place right from the start, rather than positioning each and then cutting it to size.

Cut and glue the stem into your foundation and then simply add additional stems and build up the armature from there.

Cut a ribbon, measuring it from the inside middle point to the longest stem, pointing out. This is your measuring ribbon. As you glue the twigs, move the ribbon to see whether the twigs are still the same length.

Add all other plant material once the armature is strong and stable.

floral glue

glass

Keep the glue upright in a glass. It is worth sacrificing a bit of space in your tool bag for the ease of glue use later.

skewer applicator

I use a wooden skewer as a glue applicator.

It fits perfectly into the tip of the glue tube.

how-to | # seal plant wounds with floral glue

While it is not ideal, designing without a water source is sometimes the only solution. Especially when it comes to body flowers. A tiny drop of glue will seal the flower stem wound, reducing moisture loss.

how-to | # roll and lift glue spills away

The perfect tool for lifting away any spilled glue on flowers, fabric, and tools is tacky and almost-dry glue on the tip of a skewer. Simply dab and roll to collect the spilled glue. This also works on your skin. Just dab with the applicator (wooden skewer) and roll the glue away with the tacky glue.

how-to | upcycle a comfortable wrist corsage

I save up all the plastic reels that rolls of floral tape are wrapped around and use those for wrist corsages.

Cut open the plastic inner from a floral tape roll.

Bend the white loop to open it up a bit more, until it comfortably fits around your wrist.

Gently sand the cut sections to remove all sharp edges.

Place three sections of double-sided tape on the inside of the loop and three sections on the outside.

Measure a length of ribbon to fit twice around the plastic loop, with some extra for a bow.

Fold the ribbon in half to find the midpoint. Open the ribbon and remove the protective covering from the double-sided tape. Start to glue the midpoint of the ribbon to the inside middle of the loop. Tape the ribbon to the loop around the open edges, meeting in the middle of the outside loop, leaving some ribbon to dangle loosely.

Secure the opposite side. Tie the ribbon ends in a decorative knot or bow.

Fit the bracelet and adjust if needed. It should just hug the wrist.

Glue in the floral material.

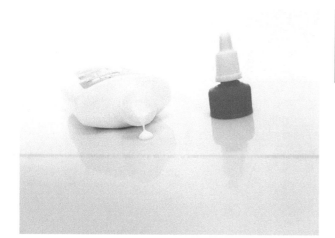

wood glue

how-to | # water down glue to soak bark

Rip the bark into long strips.

Pour out some wood glue over the strips, and then thin the glue with warm water.

Push the bark down into the warm glue and water to soak.

Wrap silver wire around a foam wreath frame and add a loop to make it easier to hang the wreath.

Wrap a soaked bark strip around the wreath frame and secure it with decorative wire.

Keep adding strips of bark. Each time, let the bark slightly overlap the previous strip. Secure the bark by wrapping decorative wire around the frame.

Wrap about half of the frame in bark strips and secure the wire with a twist.

Set the wreath aside to dry overnight.

how-to | # make papier mâché

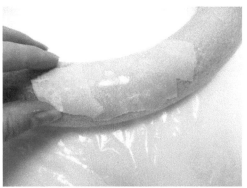

Soak some torn newsprint paper in a mixture of warm water and wood glue. Cover the foam wreath frame. Set aside to dry.

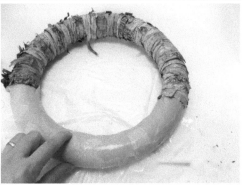

how-to | # fluff cotton flat

Pull cotton from their pods.

Gently fluff out the cotton to find the seed.

Gently pull the fluff from the seed without ripping it.

This creates a flat disk of cotton fluff that radiates outward from the seed.

Glue the cotton disks to the wreath frame by adding a small drop of wood glue to the back of the disk right where the seed is.

Overlap the disks slightly.

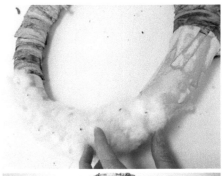

how-to | # frost twigs

Pour out a few drops of wood glue onto the twigs.

Sprinkle artificial snow over the glue to fall naturally. You can even add bits of glitter in the snow to add a twinkle.

Set aside to dry. The glue dries clear, leaving only the snowflakes visible.

wire

how-to | # cover wire with paper

Roll a section of paper raffia flat. Paint the paper raffia with wood glue. Cover the wire with the raffia, twisting it to secure.

Paper covered wire makes great bind wire.

The dried wood glue acts as a stiffener while the wire remains pliable. This means the paper wire keeps its shape perfectly.

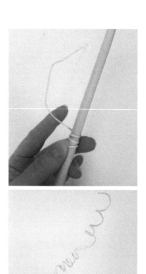

how-to | # wind wire tendrils

Curl wire around a wooden skewer, dowel, or pencil (depending on how big you want the tendril curls), leaving sections straight at irregular intervals to create a natural-looking tendril.

| # protect soft wire from plier tooth marks

Even long-nose pliers without grooves can damage soft aluminum wire. Cover the pliers' teeth with the smallest adhesive bandage, pad-side in.

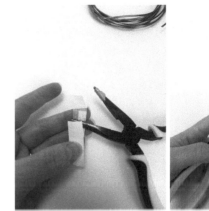

| # Unravel wire from a copper pot scrubber

Unroll the knitted wire tube. Tug the end piece and start to unravel. This wire can also be curled with a knife or scissors as you would gift ribbon. Gently pull the wire over the blunt side of your knife.

| # roll wire baubles

Roll the wire into a ball.

Roll the ball between your palms. Start by rolling lightly to make a large, loose ball. The harder you roll the ball, the smaller and tighter the result.

| # twist beaded wire

Thread beads into the wire. For larger beads, wrap the wire around the bead and thread it back through. For smaller beads, simply twist the wire to keep the beads in place.

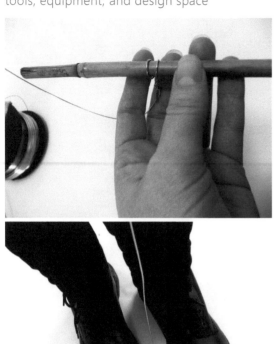

how-to | # straighten wire

Wire is always sold in a roll, and it can be very frustrating to remove bends, kinks, and curls.

Do not cut the wire from the roll. Secure the wire to a strong stick, dowel, or bamboo. Step on the stick with all your weight. As you unroll the wire, pull it upward.

Pull tightly.

The wire will now be completely straight and ready to use . . . ready to be cut, bent, and curled as you desire.

 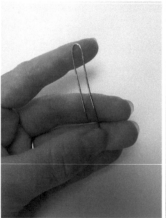  

how-to | # bend a hairpin from wire

Cut both ends of the wire at a sharp angle.

Bend the two ends together.

This is a basic hairpin wire.

For extra hold, bend the "u" part of the wire at an angle.

how-to | pin and weave a few bands to gather grass in a "just grew like this" basket

Paint a piece of Styrofoam green and fit it into a flat container.

Connect blades of grass with a small drop of glue to snugly wrap around the length of the foam.

Wiggle in blades of grass all the way around. Use hairpin wires to pin the strands to the foam to keep them upright.

Fit another loop and continue weaving.

Place the orchids in water tubes.

Press the tubes into the foam.

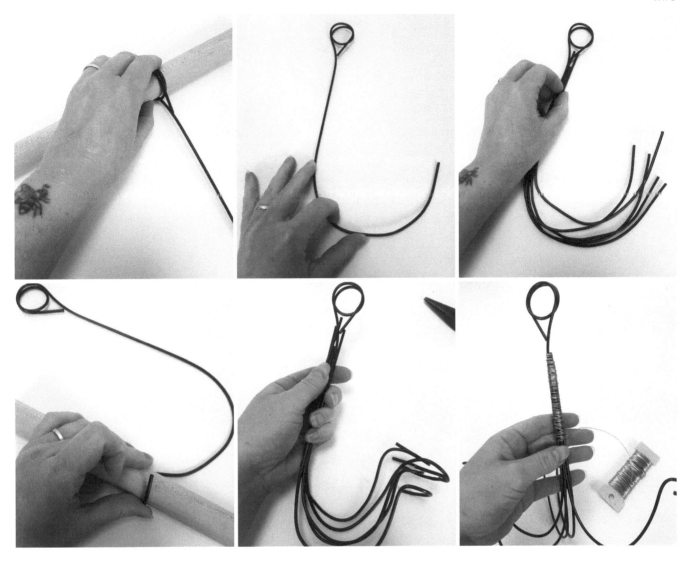

how-to | glue a spring-forest chandelier from wire and bark

The chandelier is shaped around a wire skeleton.

Shape the top of the chandelier by wrapping the end of a sturdy wire around a thick dowel. This gives your chandelier a strong place to hang.

Curve the wire to the end. I wanted my chandelier to have five curves.

Wrap the ends of the wire curves around the dowel to create the base of the battery-candle holder.

Wrap a wire around all the curves and shape it into the chandelier.

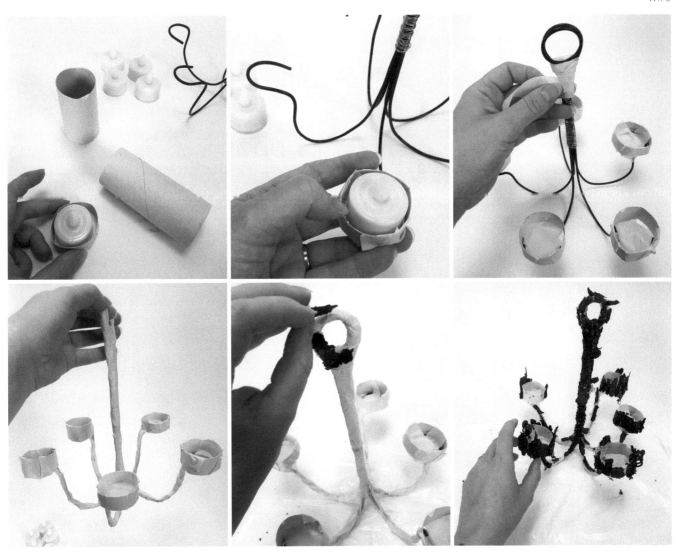

Cut a cardboard roll into sections, just bigger than the battery-powered candles.

Tape the cardboard roll on the curve of the wire base.

Cover the entire shape with masking tape or paper.

Glue bark to the chandelier to cover the tape.

Simply glue in the flowers. The kalanchoe flowers last for over a week in a design like this. I preserved the tiny ivy leaves in silica gel before adding them to the design.

ribbon, line, string, and rope

ribbon

I mostly use satin and silk ribbon. It is easy to stiffen into position with a drop of wood glue (or decoupage glue).

Prevent fraying by heating the ends either with a wire cutter, open flame, or iron.

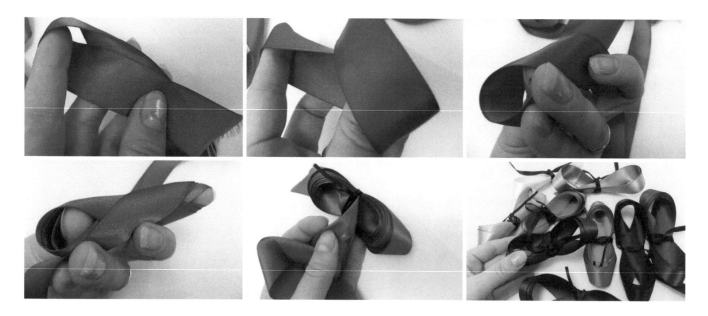

how-to | # flat-store ribbon in a figure 8

This is a great way to protect and neatly roll your ribbon, then store flat in a drawer, or take along in your tool bag.

Start the infinity fold by looping the ribbon around your finger. Loop the long, dangling ribbon around your thumb. Cross the ribbon at the back and continue to fold the infinity pattern. Continue to fold the ribbon, crossing each section at the back. Fold the last bit of ribbon to the back. Tie with a thin ribbon.

Use the ribbon from the inside end out. The loops will unwind without tangling, and there will be no fold lines in your ribbon.

how-to | make silk ribbon strands

I also unravel ribbon to make soft, silky strands. One use of these strands is to introduce a "difficult to find in nature" colour into armatures.

fishing line

A nearly invisible design solution for any project where you want the tie to be secure yet not be seen.

sisal

Sisal is a natural fiber and a convenient design solution for when you are traveling to a place where taking plant material across the border might be problematic.

Sisal is especially helpful in this type of instance when you need to prepare your design ahead of time. Sisal can be classified as "rope" and is therefore not considered plant material at border control. On top of that, sisal can be considered "ripped, and not machined" plant material, which can be more acceptable in competitions.

The word *sisal* either refers to the common name of the agave plant or the fibers that is made from ripping the plant leaf. Each leaf has on average 1,000 fibers. It is inexpensive and readily available.

I use sisal as twine to tie things and unravel sisal to create barely-there armatures. It soaks up glue in no time, is completely rigid once the glue sets, is easy to colour with natural dye, and it is really tough.

rope

how-to | make rope: basic cordage

Any plant with long fibers (bark, pods, fruits, or leaves) can be used to make rope. I used ripped phormium (flax, New Zealand flax) in this picture.

Scrape the fibers so that the long, white strands are visible. Buff the material a bit by roughing it up to make it fluffy. If I were making rope, I would probably remove all the green pulp. But for floral art, I like the little wildness of imperfection, so I leave some on for a handmade look.

Twist the strands lightly into a long strand. Simply combine sections and twist together.

Fold the strand in half and hook it over something. I used a dowel in the picture, but I hook it around a drawer handle in my design room when making longer strands.

Separate the strands. Twist-roll the strand on your right away from you and pull it forward and over the left strand. The left strand is now on your right. Twist-roll it and pull it over the left strand.

Continue down the strand to combine it and knot both ends.

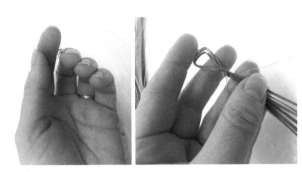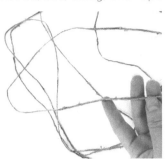

how to | # wrap a beaded, copper-wire flax strand

Rip a few fibrous leaves into strips. Twist beads into a wire.

Gather and wrap the strips with beaded wire.

how-to | # weave a beaded coil carpet

Twist wires together in the middle and weave the beaded flax strand around the wire to spiral out. Secure by twisting the wire ends back into the flax and pinch with pliers.

knots

how-to

how-to | tie a granny knot

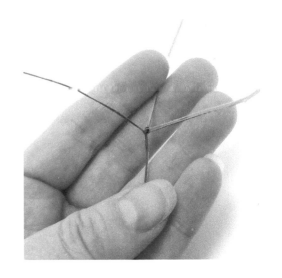

This is everyone's go-to knot. It is also called a shoelace knot for obvious reasons.

For such fine knotting as this, you need no more than two uncomplicated granny knots.

For a more permanent hold, try making the knot more than once. The strongest hold is knotting it three times—first in one direction, then again in the same direction, and lastly in the opposite direction. You can also secure it permanently with a drop of wood glue right on the knot.

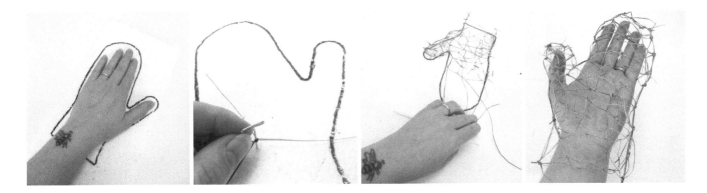

how-to | knot ripped flax mittens

Draw the mitten pattern on Styrofoam.

Knot two sections of ripped flax and pin them to the Styrofoam.

Add a few more flax strands and knot them together, like the way lace is built up, following the pattern.

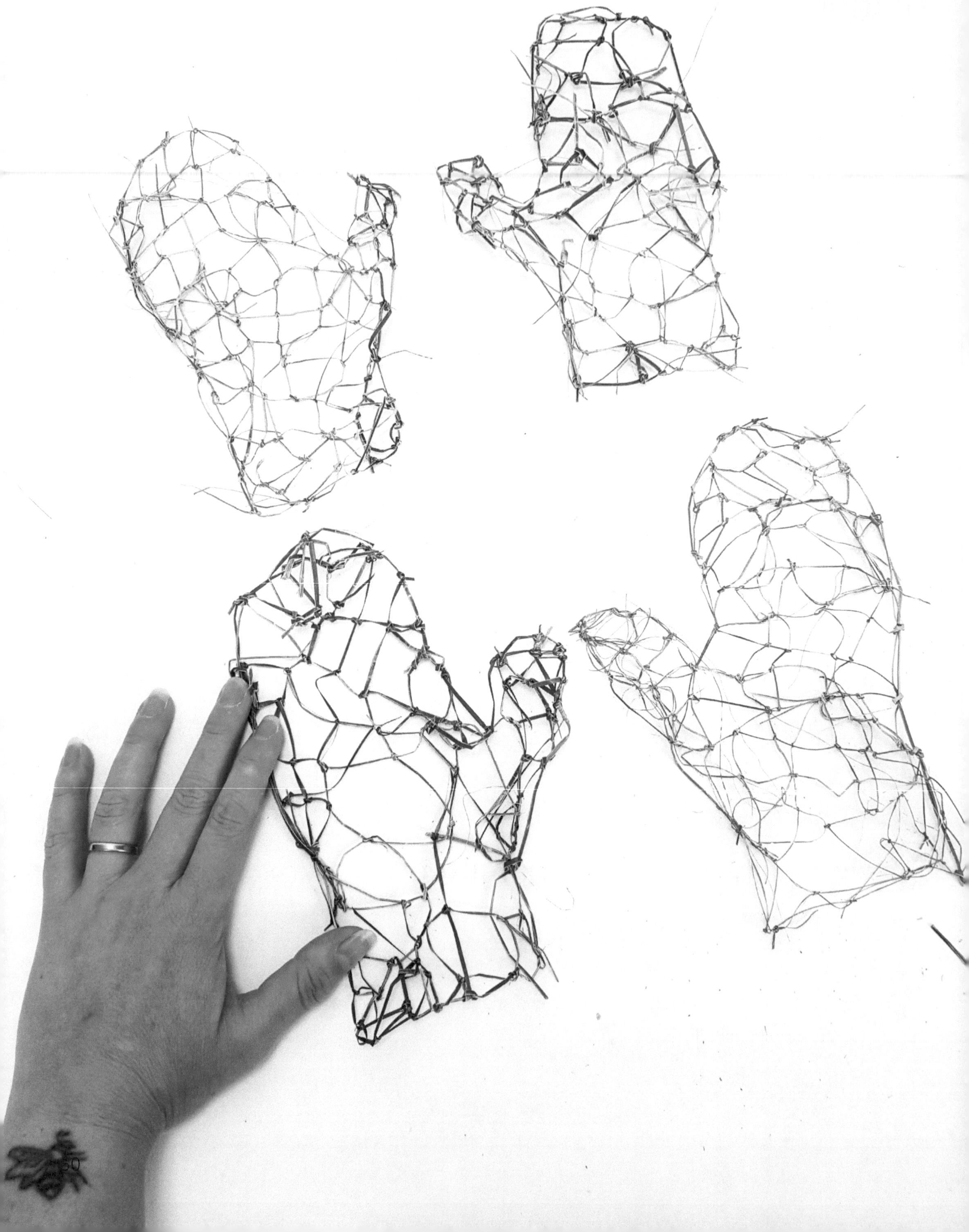

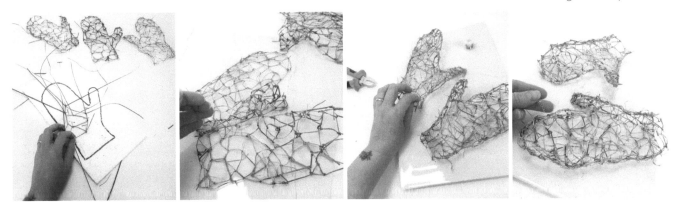

Make a second mitten. Then make two more mittens for the other hand.

Once you have all four mittens knotted, match them together in pairs.

Stitch a pair together with wire. The wire makes it easier to shape the mittens so that they puff out rather than lie flat.

Shape the mitten and add a few wire tendrils, and dewdrop crystals for sparkle. Repeat for the second mitten.

how-to | place flowers in the bottom layer of the mittens

Carefully place flowers in the bottom layer to add depth to the design. Gently fold the petals up and grasp the flower with flat-paddle tweezers, so that the petals don't get bruised.

Apply floral glue and position the flower.

how-to | tie a constrictor knot

Fold two loops into a figure 8.

Fold the loops away from you and slip over the object you want to tie closed. Pull the ends to tighten.

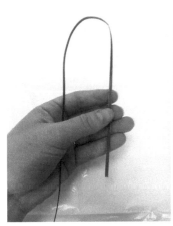   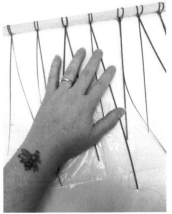

how-to | # tie a lark's head knot

I use this knot whenever I need to hang designs. It is also called a bale sling knot.

Fold the grass in half with a loop at the center.

Take the loop and slide it around a dowel or stick, so that you can see the ends through the loop.

Take the two ends and pass them through the loop.

Pull it tight.

  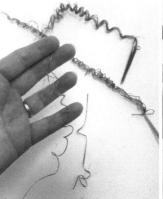 

how-to | # curl ripped flax into ringlets

Wrap the ripped flax around a dowel and clip it to secure.

Set it aside to dry.

Unroll the flax.

how-to | tie an overhand knot

Make a loop in the grass. Loop the grass back, crossing it over the loop and pressing it through the loop.

Pull the ends to tighten.

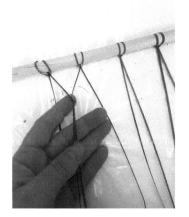

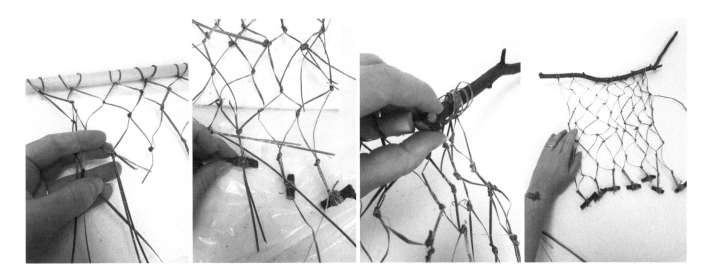

how-to | knot a fishing net

With a lark's head knot, tie a few blades of grass to a dowel.

Let the first blade and the last blade remain unknotted until the second row of knots.

Split the grass, and knot two adjacent blades. Move down the dowel and knot all the grass stems.

When you reach the second row, knot the first blade and continue. To add a new blade, fold the strip in half and loop it over the previous knot, then tie with a lark's head knot.

For my design, I transferred the net to a twig, and ended it by winding the blades to dangling twigs to give it some weight so that it hangs straight.

how-to | tie a gathering knot

To make it easier to see how it's done, I am showing how to make a gathering knot around a dowel.

Make a loop in the grass.

Bend the grass up toward the one end.

Wrap over the loop.

When you get to the end of the loop or end of the blade of grass, catch the grass through the loop.

Pull the other end so that the loop closes up, then secure the knot.

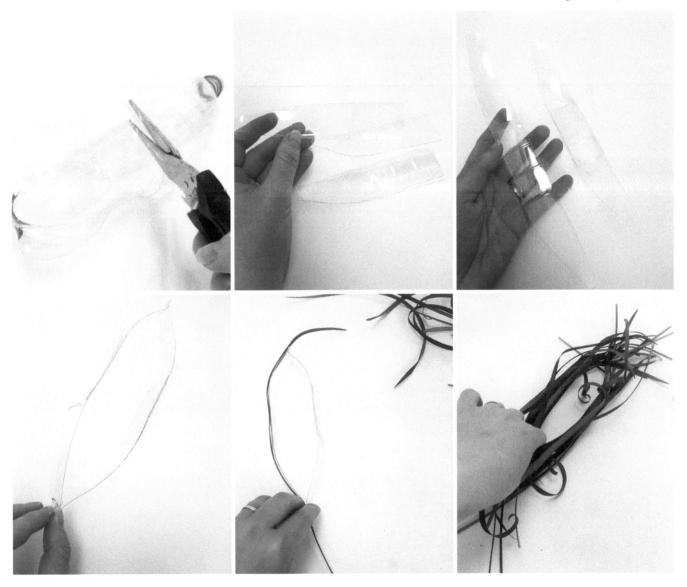

how-to | craft a cupped grass tangle

Rinse out a two-liter soda bottle and cut it open. Cut four strips out of the plastic from the middle point up to the neck.

Glue the four strips with hot glue so that you have two strips overlapping the middle sections. Glue the top and bottom ends.

Follow the plastic shape by gluing in some lily grass. Build up the lily grass, one blade at a time, to cover the plastic shape. Curl a few blades of grass, and glue it into the armature.

Secure with a gathering knot at the top and bottom, and add fresh flowers. I placed these dendrobium orchids in drinking straw water tubes.

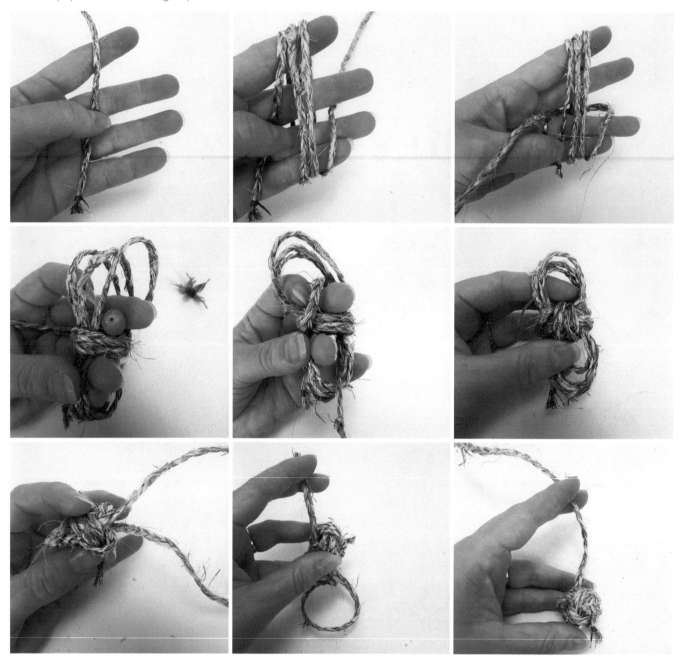

how-to | tie a monkey's fist knot

Working in three strands, wrap the strand of string three times.   Wrap a strand of string around your fingers. On completion of the third wrap, change direction and wrap the strand around the three strands of string.

On completion of the third wrap, change direction again. Slip a berry, nut, or rose hip into the hole, and wrap the string over and under the horizontal three strands.

On completion of the third wrap, keep holding the end point, and find the beginning point. Pull the strand, working in reverse, to feed it back through the loops to pull it tight.

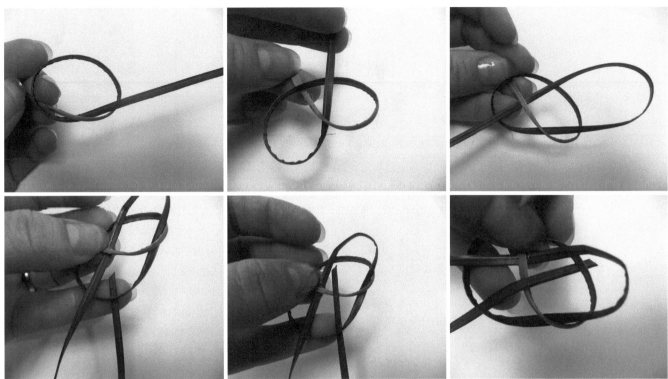

how-to | tie a heart knot

This is a traditional Celtic craft knot. Only, I am not tightening the foliage knot.

Make a knot from a blade of grass, palm, or a section of ripped flax, as I did here.

Bend both ends up, pointing to the top.

Bend the right leg in and weave it under the middle blade of grass. Pull the blade end through the knot.

Bend the blade and weave it under the outside loop of the knot.

Weave the blade over the inside knot, then under the next piece, and over and out to complete the knot.

Bend the middle point at the bottom at a sharp angle. Then wiggle and pull the knot tighter to shape the heart.

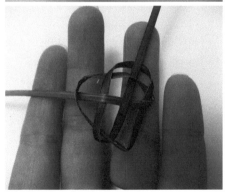

design space

My energy level is greatly affected by my design space. Due to the nature of my work, my small design room is set up to be part photography studio, and part design space. But it is a small space. I am a minimalist at heart and do not like clutter. I prefer to start with a blank canvas. My ideal would be what most people describe as a cold and sterile environment, but the reality is that this is a working space and I will likely never maintain my perfect space for long. Nevertheless, I try—but rarely succeed—to keep my space as close to my ideal working environment as possible. If the clutter runs away from me, I get overwhelmed and frustrated, and my art stops happening.

Create a design space in which you do your best work, an environment that sets you up to succeed. Things to consider:

- Is your design table at a comfortable height for you to work at?

- Do you have to carry heavy buckets a long way just because you have not fixed that thing next to the basin?

- Do you have a cool spot to design in? Cool tools? Don't underestimate the power of feeling kinda cool and bad-ass when you are out there doing your stuff and making that effort to appear effortless.

- Finish all those half-done projects. Fix that glaring light bulb.

- Get a space that is always ready. Where you can photograph your designs at any moment. This way you can celebrate with a photo when the results are better than what you thought possible.

You are a craftsman mastering a craft. Adding your contribution to a craft form that is as old as creativity. What you have and what you use should reflect that.

working surface

Set up a working surface that excites you. Don't just make do.

Your working surface should be as large as the space allows and always ready to use or ready to set up quickly so that you do not need to delay your creativity and prepare a space when inspiration hits you.

If you do not have a permanent space for designing, consider getting something that folds up when you are not working. This way your working space will not be used for anything else when you are not working—no temptation to mess up your surface with non-work-related clutter.

Make sure your working surface is at the right height for you. If you spend long hours standing, get yourself a working table with a low rack slightly lifted from the floor. Placing one foot on the rack helps to alleviate backaches. Think about your body as it works. What can you do to better support it as you work, increasing your comfort so that your creativity is not encumbered by physical limitations or barriers?

lights

The quality of light where you work is important. Let's start with the natural light available in the space. Notice the light quality and content as-is, without any additional light sources or props.

Now, consider how you can add to that natural foundation. Ideally you need light from the middle top, back left, and back right. I have three adjustable lights that I can move, and place as required.

photography background

It is convenient to have some kind of ready-to-use backdrop, if you want to take pictures of your designs in your work area (I'm just going to assume that you do, though I will explain more about the importance of photography as I go along).

I chose a crisp white for my background. White is not ideal for all my projects, but I decided a uniform look to my pictures is worth the extra effort it takes to set up some delicate designs against the stark white.

Again, your photograph space should be clean and ready to use or set up at any time. Don't spend creative energy having to fuss around with preparations, unless those preparations are part of the creative process and add to the design.

I used to have a cloth background, but floral crafting is messy work. I now buy a roll of professional photographers' paper and unroll it as needed. When I do really messy work, I use a white plastic sheet to protect the surface.

I also have three bigger-than-me-sized photographers' cloth backgrounds for larger projects. One is black, one is white, and one that is a blue/green screen.

project trays

This is how I keep my working space clear and always ready to use. I load each project, with all the bits I need to complete it in a tray of its own. This way I can work on multiple projects long before I add the flowers, and I never need to deal with clutter. Simply unpack a tray, and I am ready to design.

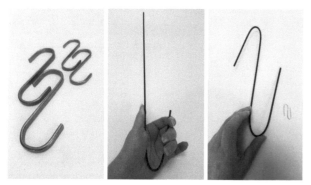

hooks to hang designs from

I have butchers' hooks in my design room that are strong enough to cope with heavy designs.

Ideally you should have two sets of hooks: two hooks to suspend designs from the top, and one hook on each side for a line, for example to hang garlands from to be photographed. You can, of course, simply bend your own hooks.

storage

When it comes to supply odds and ends, I believe you use what you see. My supplies and equipment are stored in a cupboard with glass doors, open racks under my worktable, drawers that I can pull open and see contents at a glance or clear containers, so that when I am looking for inspiration I can see what I have.

If it is packed away behind something, or in a box, I will forget about it. Out of sight, out of mind. These forgotten items are likely to get damaged. At the very least, they take up valuable space and add clutter. I also pack the things I want to upcycle, or that are particularly messy (like odd cardboard or Styrofoam shapes) in clear containers to remind me to actually use them.

After an overwhelmingly busy period, I clean out everything and give myself a fresh start. This is especially valuable if you reuse some supplies for designs. If you have a trusty piece of something that you always rely on using, pause. Maybe this piece is stopping you from exploring new ideas. It is time . . . let it go.

ladder

Not a chair or a make-do stack of something for reaching high. Get yourself a proper step ladder.

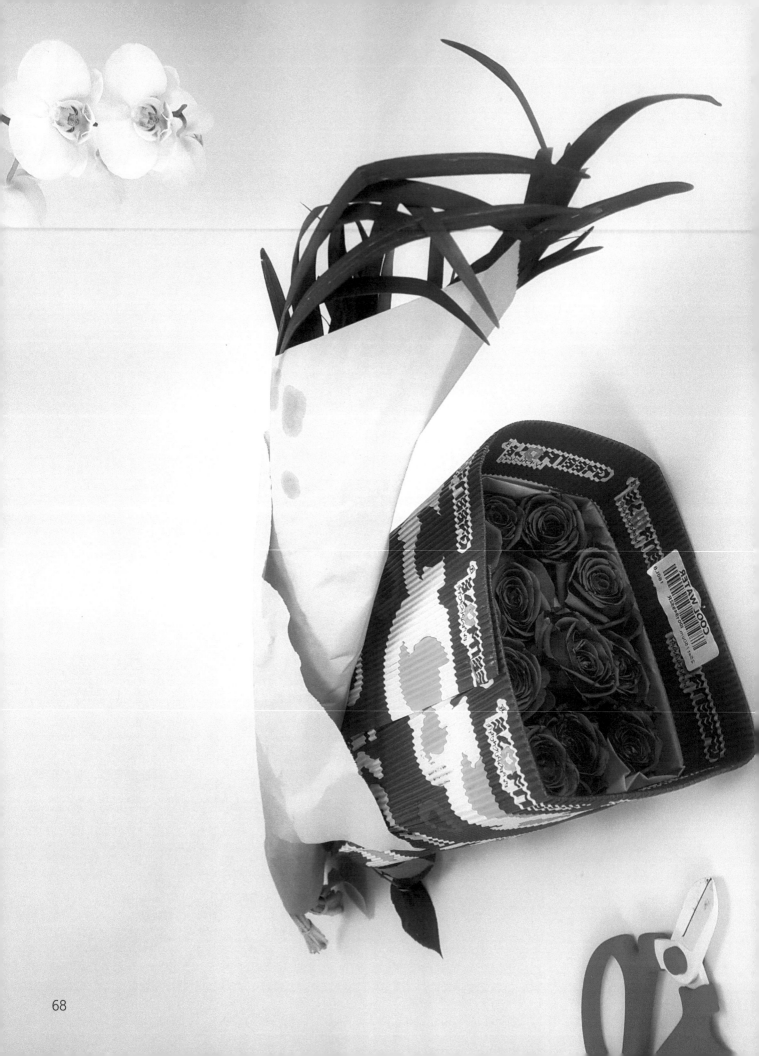

first aid for your design elements

"pay attention to the way plants look.
they will tell you all you need to know
about what they need to survive."

Conditioning is first aid for flowers experiencing trauma after being cut. Now, nothing makes for a more spirited discussion between floral crafters than the mere mention of "conditioning." It is steeped in tradition, home remedies, and even a pinch of myth and superstition.

We give it so much attention, for good reason—conditioning is the foundation of our own design philosophy as floral crafters and is the heart of all our techniques. Conditioning is how we show appreciation, gratitude, honour, and respect, making the flowers that we have crafted so carefully last as long as possible. It is also how we learn which plants are suitable for which techniques.

The different kinds of plant material we design with have unique qualities that make them particularly suitable for certain techniques. If you understand the unique conditioning needs of each, you understand how they respond to being manipulated. This book discusses more about this when we look at creating illusions, but for now: What is the best way to condition flowers? The answer is understandably complicated. Some flowers are just notoriously difficult to condition (I am looking at you, hydrangeas), and, to be honest, there are some flowers that I would just not choose for a competition design because they cannot be relied upon, no matter how carefully they are conditioned.

This chapter will show you what to look for so that your way of thinking about conditioning can transform from being complicated to being a natural response to the plant material you craft with. Ultimately, conditioning can become an effortless practice that comes naturally. The first step is to understand the trauma plants experience after they are severed from their roots.

how-to | rehydrate hydrangeas

No matter how well conditioned hydrangeas are, sometimes they just wilt prematurely.

Place the entire flower head in a water bath, and let it rest for a few hours.

It should perk up completely.

Give the stem a fresh cut and place in water, in your design.

Plants have a vascular system that works similar to a drinking straw. When you suck on a straw, you are creating a difference in air pressure between the top and the bottom of the straw, causing liquid to be pushed up the straw. In plants, the suction at the top of their vascular system is caused by evaporation of water through leaves and stems. This process is called transpiration. Just like sucking on a straw, transpiration creates a difference in air pressure (between top and bottom), which forces water up into the plant through its roots.

This process is interrupted the moment you cut the plant from its roots. The plant experiences this change as trauma. The whole point of conditioning is understanding and limiting this trauma.

Air is drawn up into the vascular system when you cut or break a plant's stem. Just think of what happens when you suck on a straw, and the bottom lifts out of the liquid, or if there is a hole in the side of the straw. The water ceases to lift up. Air in a plant's vascular system prevents it from supplying the cells with water and carbohydrates needed to stay alive.

The damaged cells at this cut now release enzymes to let the other cells know that the plant is in trouble. Wound hormones are manufactured to stop the loss of moisture by creating new cells and scar tissue.

The plant's basic instinct to reproduce takes over, and it starts to wilt, sending moisture from the leaves and stems to the reproductive areas such as flowers, fruit, and seeds. New growth is the first to show signs of wilting due to the diverted moisture because the cellular structure of these beautiful and fragile stems is not fully developed. The cells simply collapse without sufficient moisture.

To further limit moisture loss, mature foliage and all other big surface areas exposed to the elements (sun, temperature, wind) start to wilt. Finally, all plant functions are slowed and eventually stop.

soak up colour pigments using the natural vascular system of plant material

Mix a few drops of food colouring in water.

Give the flower stems a fresh cut and set in the dye solution.

Within a half hour you should begin to see the pigment colour as it is sucked up into the petals.

Rainbow flowers are created by splitting the tips of the stems and placing each tip in a different colour dye bath.

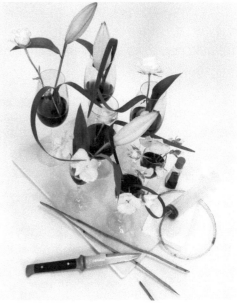

floral first aid

First and foremost, provide hydration. Get those stems into water, right now.

- ❦ Keep the vascular system open.

- ❦ Minimize additional cell damage caused by bruising and bacterial invasion.

- ❦ Feed the cells to halt trauma.

- ❦ Minimize photosynthesis to protect the remaining resources.

- ❦ Provide the best possible environmental conditions for your plant material to be suspended in this state of beauty for as long as possible.

There is no one solution that will suit all your flowers, foliage, pods, and fruits. No one plan of action will prevent trauma in all the different plants you will want to design with. The approach to floral first aid must be matched to specific plant requirements. Also, we must take into consideration where we obtain the floral material from.

Flowers from a garden, wholesalers, and florists all require different floral first aid.

Flowers we grow ourselves are the hardiest because they were exposed to the elements and were forced to develop strong cellular structures. For the same reason, the flowers may be less pronounced. Flowers bought from wholesalers are most often grown in ideal conditions, such as in greenhouses or hydroponic installations. These plants flower quickly, and in some cases so fast that the cellular structure is too weak to sustain life after the flowers wilt and die away. Others are so healthy that given the right treatment cuttings will root and happily grow again when planted.

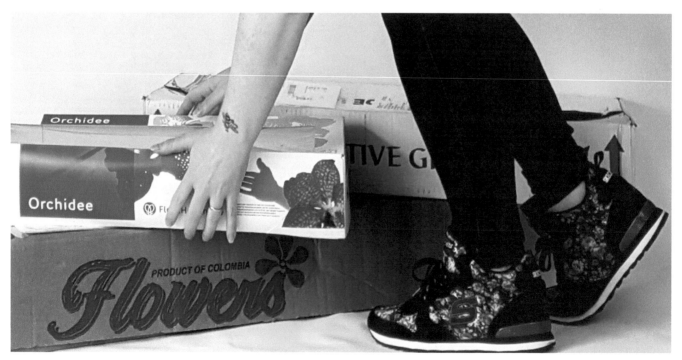

Flowers obtained from a florist are harvested days or even weeks before they are shipped to the flower shop. Both wholesaler and florist-supplied flowers have most likely been dry packed, shipped, and handled many, many times before we receive them. That means the flowers are well into the process of healing the cut and are already experiencing trauma.

Additionally, flowers suspended in cold environments, such as floral fridges, may be dehydrated and bruised in ways that are not immediately apparent, only becoming visible once they reach room temperature, as you are designing or soon after.

design note | floral fridges are not the same as home fridges

There is no air circulation nor added humidity in a home fridge, and the optimum temperatures differ. Placing flowers in your home fridge is not a good idea. Also, do not use your floral fridge to store food in. Flowers are sensitive to ethylene gas released by food, especially fruit.

Each of these situations brings its own set of floral first aid challenges. The following sections explain how to navigate them. I will start by exploring how to harvest flowers, and then the conditioning of self-harvested flowers. Floral first aid for purchased flowers starts with selection and transportation, even before conditioning them. Thereafter I will explain how to "make the cut" and other grooming needs, including designing with succulents and tillandsias. Finally, I will address preserving flowers and foliage as a lasting form of floral first aid.

how-to | secret tip for conditioning new growth

Conditioning new growth and sprouts is difficult because the little sprouts have not had time to fully develop the cellular structure necessary for taking up water after being cut. The cells will collapse within hours from severing, and the beautiful new growth will wilt, looking limp in your design. But new growth looks so fantastic that it may be tempting to include it.

My advice is to grow your own. It takes time, but it is the only way to have new growth in a design that will not wilt. Condition a sprouting twig rather than just the bright green sprout. The twig will be able to withstand being cut and will supply the sprout with water

Choose hardy stems with beautiful new growth, and condition them well before cutting and placing them into water tubes.

Remember the little twig will still think it is growing, so make sure it has access to water. You will also need to top up the water regularly.

harvesting your flowers

🌿 Harvest plant material only where you have permission to do so.

🌿 Water the plants 24 hours before harvesting. Water only the roots and not the foliage or flowers.

🌿 If you prefer, spray with natural bug deterrent spray 24 hours in advance. This is not necessary because most bugs will be long gone after the harvesting, conditioning, and grooming process. But if you want to spray, it really is better to try a natural solution (such as chrysanthemum tea) rather than a poisonous pesticide.

🌿 Early in the morning or early in the evening is the best time for harvesting flowers. Cut the plant material with a clean, sharp blade.

🌿 Be generous with your stem allowance. You can always cut the stem shorter when designing.

🌿 Cut responsibly. As a rule of thumb, cut as you would when you prune. Do not cut more than you will actually need, and never cut in such a way that you destroy the plant.

🌿 Place your harvest in water as soon as possible.

🌿 Do not overcrowd the bucket with flowers and foliage.

🌿 Protect your harvest from sun, heat, wind, and overhandling.

first aid for your design elements

how-to | craft a double wreath with quince blossoms

Cut three branches to create legs for the wreaths to stand on.

Wire the branches to the largest wreath.

Wire the smaller wreath to the larger wreath.

Add the blossom branches into the design.

Keep the blossoms hydrated by placing the stems in large water tubes.

Glue in a few sparkling beads and grapevine tendrils.

how-to | ## give any container a barrel hitch knot handle to make it easy to carry your stems home

Place the container on the ribbon or string.

Bring the ribbon over the container and make a knot.

Open the knot slightly and slip it over the rim of the container.

Pull the ribbon ends up, catching on the knot. The heavier the container, the tighter the knot will pull.

how-to | # carry a bundle of stems

Cut two straight-ish twigs.

Measure the ribbon width against the twig. Score a line with a sharp knife. Peel the bark away that falls under the ribbon lines that you marked. Do so on both ends of both twigs. This will keep the ribbon in place.

Tie ribbon to one twig to rest over this stripped section in a double granny knot to secure. Tie another ribbon length on the same twig on the other side.

Extend the ribbon out and tie each ribbon to the same side on the other twig.

Place your bundle of twigs to extend over both ends of the tied ribbon.

Lift the two twigs. Slip the smaller twig through the ribbon on both sides to catch.

Lift the bundle.

conditioning your harvest

- Separate the flowers by type. Some flowers need special attention.

- Give heavy flower heads extra support.

- Make sure they have enough water and admire from a distance for at least four hours, preferably overnight, before washing, grooming, or handling. This will prevent bruising and allows the plants to settle.

- You can start the grooming, and ultimately the designing process, when your plant material is fully hydrated.

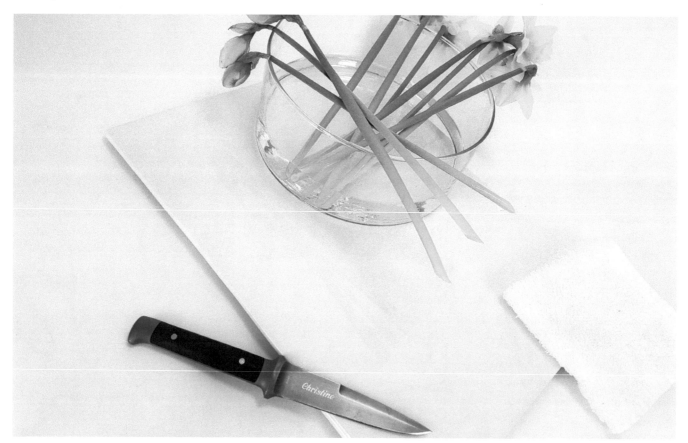

how-to | # take special care when conditioning daffodils

Daffodils (Narcissus) should always be conditioned separately. The Alkaloids (Narciclasine) in Narcissus mucilage are toxic to most other flowers (Iris is an exception,) because the sugars and polysaccharids increase bacterial growth and block water intake.

Also avoid arranging them with other flowers. If you really, really want to arrange daffodils with other flowers, make sure you condition them separately. Add special daffodil flower food so that most of the sap is removed before adding it to a mixed vase.

Change the water regularly.

design note | # let's get controversial

🌿 Do not crush woody stems. Rather give the stem a fresh cut, at an angle, to increase surface exposure. The goal is to keep the cell structure open and healthy enough to absorb moisture and limit trauma.

🌿 Do cut, or do not cut, the stems under water. It really is up to you. This does make for some interesting conversations with designers. Some believe cutting the stems under water will prevent further air bubbles entering the stem because the blade squishes the water pockets inside of the stem like a sponge, forcing it to draw up air, and again water, once released. Other designers say that the plant was not cut under water when harvested so air is already drawn up into the stem, making little to no difference now. For me it is situational, depending on the condition, and level of trauma of the flower.

🌿 Rose thorns. I love seeing thorns on rose stems, yet the biggest complaint from designers is that they "have" to remove all those thorns. This quite honestly baffles me. Yes, of course we remove the thorns when designing a wedding bouquet. Leave them on if you are selling or designing a bunch of roses. They are beautiful. Every rose has its thorn, and all that. If you must, nip away the sharpest tip, but why create more wounds than necessary? You can probably guess that I would also not agree with scraping the stems with a blade to get rid of the thorns, smoothing off the bumps, and removing old plant scar tissue. A rose with its thorns is natural and imperfections beautiful. Let it be.

🌿 Flower food. Again, tricky! I believe commercial flower food is best. It has been researched and perfected. I also add a bit of bleach to submerged designs but nothing else. Some designers believe in a copper coin added to the water, as the copper acts as an antibacterial agent. Hairspray, vodka, soda, aspirin, and sugar are also believed to make flowers last longer. I feel home remedies can introduce more bacteria or clog the vascular system of the plant, doing more harm than good. Other designers argue that we know a plant's vascular system halts all processes when in trauma, so flower food of any kind will have little to no effect, and hydration alone is enough.

Find your own way. Consider your experiences and develop your own design philosophy.

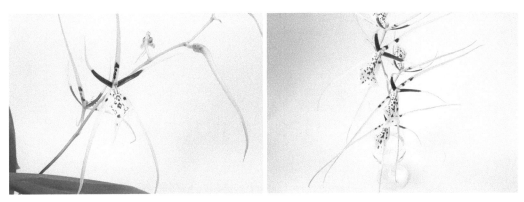

design note | Bruises do not heal

Tropical flowers with bruises or cuts deteriorate fast, and it will only become more obvious after you have carefully conditioned the flowers.

84

selecting your flowers

Find a supplier who is as passionate about the condition of the flowers and plant material they sell, as you are about designing. We have all purchased a plant in full bloom that, despite our best efforts, just wilted and died once the flowers faded. This is usually caused by artificial growth acceleration by growers to get flowering plants to the market as quickly as possible. Over-hybridizing, intense fertilizers, and growth hormones are some of the growth-stimulating methods used, resulting in plants that develop at such a rate that they are simply not strong enough to last. You should also be aware of where your flowers are harvested. Some growers use carcinogenic pesticides and herbicides, and unsustainable methods. Some plants are harvested in such a way that the roots are damaged and the plant simply dies, while others are overharvested. For example, many Lady Slipper orchids are endangered and on the verge of extinction in the wild due to incorrect and over harvesting.

As floral craftsmen, we need to educate ourselves, do our research, and view supporting conscientious and sustainable suppliers as part of our design philosophy.

For the best results, purchase high-quality flowers, just before they peak. Small and weak cut flowers will not improve with love and care. You also know now how to spot trauma. Look at any new growth—if it is limp, it is too late. Inspect the foliage to determine the age of the flowers. Foliage that is wilted or diseased is obviously not a good choice. Look out for clever tricks used to suspend flowers past their prime. Ask questions. If the foliage has been removed altogether, or the stems were heat treated, be wary. Peek into the buckets to see if the water is clean and smells fresh.

Select flowers according to when you intend to design with them. Flowers with too tight buds might not open, whereas flowers in full bloom (showing an "open" colour) are best designed with within 24 hours. Select stems that are somewhere in between for longer lasting flowers.

It is always a good sign if your grower, supplier, or florist does more than "just enough" to get the flowers sold. Look for places that supply flower food with purchases, have flower head supports on heavier blooms like gerbera daisies, and provide a net, cardboard sleeve, or wire to protect the flowers from bruising.

A good supplier will not sell epiphytes (such as orchids growing in bark) planted in soil or combine plants with a low water requirement in the same pot as a plant that needs to remain wet.

Your flower supplier is a valuable resource and will provide advice on how to further grow or condition your plant material.

how-to | support heavy flower heads

Heavier flower heads can be wired or supported by slipping the stem into a plastic straw.

transporting your flowers

Oh ... stress! At least 70 percent of my competition or event design stress comes from transportation, getting to and from the venue.

- Prepare the delivery vehicle in advance to make sure you have adequate space.

- Regulate the vehicle's temperature so that it is suitable for the flowers.

- Do not expose the flowers to exhaust or gas fumes. Nor to heat, direct sun, or wind from open windows.

- To prevent spills, do not overfill a bucket (or vase) used for transporting flowers. Secure the container so that it does not topple over in transit. Also, support the heads of the flowers so that they do not break from the movement.

- I find the best way is to pack the flowers flat in a box, preferably with some sort of a water source.

- Pack the flowers immediately before you leave.

- Experiment with what works   for you.

86

how-to | flat-pack flowers in a box

Flowers and foliage might move around and get damaged in transit. To secure, make two holes in the bottom of the box and thread wire, elastic bands, or cable ties through to tie the flower stems or design to the box. You can also tape the stems or the water source to the box.

If needed, add a few ice packs to regulate the temperature. Wet newspaper wrapped around the stems will also help regulate the temperature if you do not have an ice pack.

Line the box with plastic or foam to make it waterproof.

Place shredded paper, cotton, or wadded tissue paper in the box to cushion the flowers.

Staple or glue vertical and horizontal blocks of wood in the box to act as support in case something heavy falls or rests on it.

Place the flowers in a water tube or some other water source, and only pack the flowers into the box at the last possible moment.

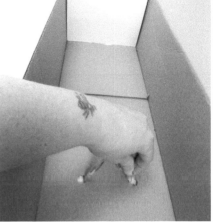
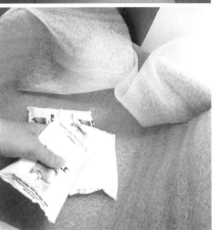

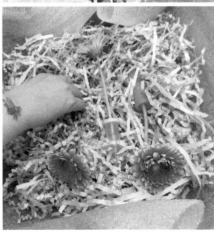

conditioning your purchase

Flowers from your florist are obviously older than flowers from your garden and should therefore be conditioned differently. Florist flowers already have had some time to stabilize from the original trauma of being cut. If conditioned correctly by the florist, their stem and vascular systems will again be open, nourishing the flowers.

The healing process will, however, also have begun, progressively sealing the stem's vascular tissue where it was cut. Remove this by giving the stems a fresh cut, at an angle, about 2.5 cm (1 in) above the previous cut or above any damage. You can make this cut under water or not, as you prefer.

It is up to you to provide the ideal environment for your flower purchase, so ensure that you understand the unique demands of each plant you plan to design with.

The following notes can serve as a guide.

design note | # as a rule of thumb

- Tropical flowers that bloom in warmer climates or seasons prefer warmer water.

- Cool weather flowers need to be hydrated in cooler water and will open faster in warmer water.

- Warm weather flowers, such as roses, that have been refrigerated respond well to a drink of warm water so that the cold vascular system can heat up and take up water.

- In most cases, removing excess foliage from stems conserves moisture and prolongs the flower's life. It is especially important to avoid bacterial growth by removing all foliage that falls below the waterline.

- If a flower is supported, leave this support on until the flower is plump and hydrated.

- Trim or pick away foliage carefully to avoid further wounds that could cause trauma, moisture loss, or bacteria to enter the vascular system.

- Handle flowers as little as possible to avoid bruising the petals. Only groom the flowers after they are completely hydrated.

- Place flowers in a cool, low-light location until they are plump and hydrated.

how-to | condition chrysanthemums

Condition as you would any semi-woody stems, leaving some foliage on the stem, above the waterline. The foliage will help draw moisture up to the flower heads.

making the cut

how-to

cut spiked flower stems

Orchids grow in long flower spikes.

Cut the flower from the main stem just where the stems connect.

Cut the stem at an angle.

This creates a neat cut without appearing like it was artificially shortened, but rather as if the flowers naturally grew on a short stem that opened all the way to the top.

how-to

cut tulips

You will notice a white end on all tulip stems. This is where the stem snaps when the growers pull the flowers from the bulbs when harvesting. This white area is firm and prevents the stem from losing moisture; it also prevents the flower from taking up moisture. Cut the stem at an angle just above the white area.

how-to	# cut bamboo

Cut bamboo stems just above, or well below, a node, so that it can still take up water.

how-to	# cut carnations

Cut carnation stems just above the node. This ensures that the flower stem can still take up water.

how-to	# bite and snap a sturdy twig

Let your cutters bite into the twig.

Rotate the stem just a little and let your cutters again bite into the stem.

Repeat this process to create a neat score line.

Break the twig neatly on the score line.

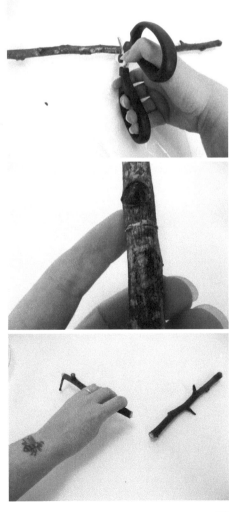

how-to | caramalize milky stems

When cut, some stems exude a milky sap that is messy and can be an irritant if it gets on your skin. Give the stem a clean cut and rinse it under running water. If there is still some liquid running from the wound, you need to burn it over a flame for a few seconds, to seal and caramelize it. Place the stem in warm water to condition.

how-to | choose, cut and condition hellebore

What we call petals on hellebores are actually sepals that protect the tiny flower. If you look carefully at the flower, you will notice tiny petals that surround the stamens. These sepals become increasingly hardy as the flower matures.

Wait for the flower to be pollinated before picking. When the tiny petals and stamens drop, and the seedpod develops, you can harvest and successfully condition the flowers. Readiness is not necessarily indicated by the size of the sepals.

A mature and fully developed hellebore is also ideal for body flowers and will last for almost a day without water.

Dip the stem in boiling water for a few seconds before designing with it. Remember to protect the flower from the steam.

how-to | place water-soaked cotton in hollow stems

Hold the stem upside down and fill with water.

Plug the cavity with water-soaked cotton before designing.

how-to | # pull moss

Keep moss in a bag so that it remains moist, and simply pull or tear bits by hand as needed. It looks more natural than if you cut the moss into bits. Mist the moss with water when it starts to dry.

how-to | # cut flax leaves from a plant

Always cut the leaves from the outside in.

Try not to harvest the inside leaf, so that the plant continues to grow.

You can also propagate the plant by keeping these divisions in water. New roots will appear just below the crown.

how-to | # harvest cyclamen from a plant

Gently tuck the cyclamen flower or leaf from the plant by pulling the stalk upwards. The entire stem will snap off and pull out easily and cleanly. That way you will not damage any of the other healthy leaves or flowers and not disturb or hurt the tuber. You now have a nice long stem to design with.

special grooming needs

how-to | remove stamens

The best time to tug a pollen-covered head (stamen) away from the filament is when it starts to open and before pollination (puffy and yellow).

Do not cut the stamen away, as this leaves a brown mark.

how-to | fix pollen in place

Most of the time I gently tug the pollen-covered stamens away as described previously, but the gloriosa looks rather pretty with the stamens on, so I fix them in place.

Make a mask by cutting a slit into a sheet of paper.

When the stamens are pollinated (puffy and yellow), slip a few stamens at a time into the paper mask.

Set the pollen in place by spritzing the stamens with hairspray or a fixative (used to fix pastel or charcoal sketches).

Allow the hairspray/fixative to dry.

how-to | # remove messy lily pollen

Things get really messy once the stamens are pollinated.

Use a tweezer to tug the anthers (the top bit of the stamen that holds the pollen) from the stamen and place them on a paper towel that can be folded and composted.

how-to | # pick up lily pollen

Dropped pollen stains fabric and fingers.

Do not wipe. Wiping only rubs the pollen deeper into the stained fabric. Shake out any loose pollen, and then lift the remaining pollen with sticky tape.

Wrap sticky tape around your fingers, sticky side out, and pat the pollen gently, using a fresh piece of the tape for each dab.

If there is still a yellow stain, place the fabric, stained-side down, on a paper towel and treat with dry-cleaning fluid or powder.

Wash the fabric in the hottest water that is safe for the fabric.

how-to | # lift tiny bits of dropped pollen from flowers

Wet a brush and shake off most of the water so that the brush is damp.

Dab to pick up any tiny bits of pollen, even those deep within the petals.

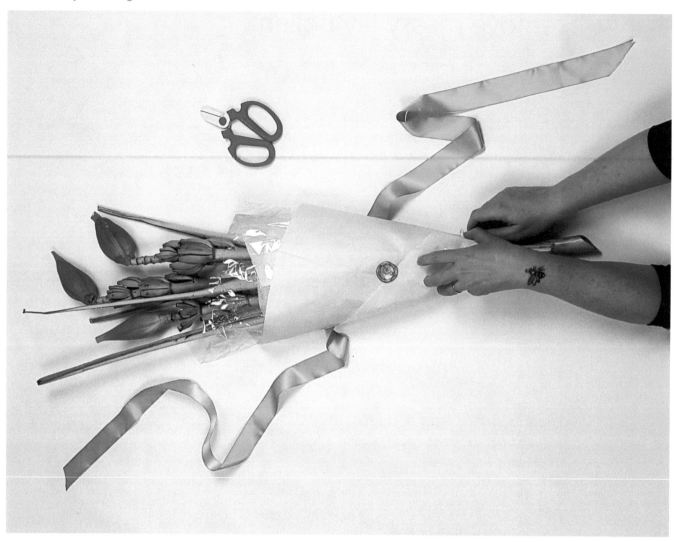

how-to | fight botrytis

Botrytis is that fuzzy grey mold found on decaying vegetative matter. It is Mother Nature's way of recycling our beautiful flowers by breaking them down as nutrients to feed growing plants. But it is a frightful sight for floral designers!

Left untreated, botrytis spores spread from the dead or decaying plant matter to living plant tissue, prematurely spoiling the entire bunch. Roses are particularly vulnerable to botrytis.

Start by inspecting the flowers you purchase. Do not buy flowers that show early signs of botrytis. You will notice tiny raised spots that become rust-coloured blotches and finally fluffy grey mold.

The best approach is to ensure sufficient airflow between blooms. Do not store flowers in their shop sleeves for long because condensation will build up inside the wrap. Also, do not overcrowd your conditioning or design spaces.

Not all flowers benefit from a misting of water because drops can get trapped deep between the petals, creating the ideal environment for botrytis spores.

how-to | perk up roses

Tiny air bubbles travel up the rose stems, causing the neck of the flower head to bend, droop, or look wilted prematurely.

Remove foliage that will fall below the conditioning waterline, and give the stem a fresh cut, at a sharp angle, with a very sharp blade (some designers even suggest that you cut the stem under water to make sure you don't introduce even more bubbles). Leave some foliage on the stem to help with the absorption of water. The foliage sucks water up the stem.

Pour about 3.5 cm (1.5 in) of boiling water in a heat-proof container.

Dip the rose stem into the boiling water, taking care to protect the flowers from the steam with paper or cloth. Keep the stem in the water for 30 seconds to 1 minute.

You will see the bubbles leaving the stem.

Remove the stem from the boiling water and give it a fresh cut. It is easy to see where to cut because the stem treated with boiling water will become discoloured. Cut about 2.5 cm (1 in) above this discolouration, at an angle, with a sharp blade, preferably under water.

If this heat-treated stem is not cut away, it will discolour even more, making it easy to see.

Pour flower food (according to the package specifications) into fresh, room-temperature water, and place the stem into the water. Set aside to rehydrate. This will take about 1 to 1.5 hours.

The stems will be firm and perked up, and you would be able to enjoy your roses for a little while longer.

Do not submerge roses in water, nor mist them, as this causes botrytis, reducing the roses' life.

how-to | # tap away pollen

Turn the flower upside down and gently tap with your ring finger.

All the pollen will drop.

how-to | # attach plant material to a stick to give it a stem

Some design ingredients need to be attached to sticks to be included in a design.

You can use wire, string, or elastic bands.

how-to | # lessen the smell of garlic- and onion-related flowers

Cut the stem at an angle in mouth rinse. This will lessen the intensity of the onion or garlic smell in the design. Place the allium stems in their own test tubes before adding them to the design.

how-to | # tidy up foliage

Mimic nature when you need to detail a plant or cut away some brown tips on a leaf. Cut the leaf in a sharp or rounded V.

Dip the scissors in lemon juice before cutting to prevent the leaf from browning.

how-to | # shine leaves

Chemical solutions are available for keeping foliage clean and shiny, but I prefer a more natural approach.

Wipe the leaf with a damp cloth, and then wipe it dry. For really shiny leaves, I dip a paper towel in olive oil and lightly buff the leaf, wiping most of the oil away.

Only shine naturally shiny leaves. The silvery-powdery or hairy covering some foliage has protects it and makes it water resistant.

how-to | # strip foliage from a weaving stem

This is the fastest way to remove all foliage from willow stems before weaving.

Wear gloves to protect your hands if you need to strip many stems. Cup your hand lightly over the stem that you want to strip, and move from the tip of the stem down, to gently remove all the leaves and side shoots. The delicate stems of new growth bend down and snap off cleanly.

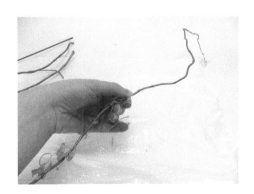

design note | water

🌾 Know your tap water. Water high in fluoride is harmful to gerberas, gladiolus, and freesias.

🌾 Soft water, which is high in sodium, is harmful to roses.

🌾 Mineral-rich water blocks the vascular system of plants and stops the plant from adequately drawing up water.

🌾 The best water for cut flowers is slightly acidic (a pH factor of between 3 and 4.5) because it is easier for the plant to draw up the water. Tap water is usually very near neutral, and you can adjust the pH by adding flower food.

🌾 Stems draw up warmer (body temperature) water faster, thereby hydrating the flowers faster.

🌾 Fill a jug with water, and let it stand while you harvest or shop for your flowers. This will allow time for all the chlorine and air bubbles to escape before the water is used for conditioning.

designing with succulents

Succulents will stay turgid in a design for quite a few days. No water source is required. In fact, succulents deteriorate fast when overwatered.

It is possible to root succulents in a design to create a long-lasting work of floral art, ever-changing as it grows. You can also propagate succulents by harvesting those shoots that are now rooted plants in your design, to grow in pots.

how-to | cut and groom succulents

Cut the succulents from the roots. Cut the stem away clean if you plan to glue the succulent into your design. Reach deep into the plant to allow for a bit more stem if you plan to wire and tape the stem into your design.

Remove any damaged or dry leaves or spent flower stems.

You can reshape the rosette by picking any leaves that are still plump and pretty. Do not discard the picked leaves because they can be propagated.

Take care not to wipe or touch the rosette too much because your fingers will remove the silvery-powdery bloom, which protects the succulent and makes it water resistant.

Set aside the plant to give the stem time to heal. The wound will start to look dry.

how-to | wire the succulent stems with a double leg mount

Create a longer stem for the succulent that can be manipulated.

Press a wire about 3 cm (1 in) through the stem and bend the shorter wire leg down.

Twist the wire around the stem and the longer wire leg. Cover the stem and wire with florist tape (gutta-percha tape). Wax on the tape melts with the heat of your fingers, securing the wire. Bend any sharp ends away for safety.

how-to | glue the succulents

Seal the wound with flower glue, and place into position. For larger rosettes, place glue on the succulent and on the object you want to glue the succulent to. Set aside until the glue becomes tacky and then bond it to the object.

designing with tillandsia

Like succulents, air plants will remain turgid in your design and do not require additional hydration, provided you keep the following guidelines in mind:

- Make sure that you mount the plant on something that will not retain water and that any water will naturally drain away to prevent fatal rot.

- Do not design in planted containers with the air plant roots in soil.

- Ocean driftwood used in designs must first be thoroughly rinsed to remove any possible salt buildup that can damage the plant.

- If you purchase wood for your design, make sure it was not treated with a copper solution. This is usually added to wood to prevent it from rotting and is toxic to air plants.

- Artificial lighting can be too harsh for air plants, negatively affecting their growth and even cause blemishes. Such lights are often used at flower shows and competitions, so pay close attention to where your design will be placed.

- Air plants require good air circulation. The ideal condition is fresh air freely moving around the plant.

- Protect air plants from magnified sunlight when designing a closed container, such as a terrarium or globe. You should also remove them from the container when you water the other plants.

Air plant roots are more for anchoring the plant to a host than for nutrient uptake, so you can cut away the roots if it is required. However, I prefer to use the roots to keep the plants in place. This has the added benefit of being able to change my design slightly every few days when I soak and replace the plants.

It is also possible to fix the plant permanently to a design, especially if the entire design can be soaked as a unit. To do that, you can either staple the roots, tie the plant with fishing line, or use a non-soluble glue. When using glue, avoid covering the entire base of the air plant because in time, the roots will regrow and naturally adhere to the design in that position.

Remember to cut or peel away any brown leaves before adding air plants to your design. The leaves can also be trimmed to suit your design, and it is best to do that at a sharp angle to mimic their natural shape.

how-to | # twig and cardboard block

Create a decorative container for an orchid and air plant by gluing snipped twigs on a square cardboard box.

Extend a few twigs toward the bottom for the block to rest on, and a few twigs toward the top for suspending the air plant above the orchid. Line the box with plastic before adding the plants.

how-to | # mindful companion planting

Every design with plants should be its own ecosystem, matched to the needs of all the plants used in the design, so that they all can flourish. One way to mix plants with different needs is to create separate environments for each within the design.

Both slipper orchids and air plants require a semi-shaded position, but their root requirements differ.

Slip the orchid plant into a plastic and tissue paper lining to make sure the plant is not in a puddle of water (and protect the cardboard) and be sure not to deprive the orchid of light on its roots. The air plant hovers over the design, suspended on twigs. This way the air plant and orchid can easily be removed to be soaked and replaced into the design.

Rosary vine (a succulent) is draped loosely over the design. Moisture from the orchid growth medium will encourage it to root. You can plant it out in soil and add another vine to the design to root.

how-to | take care of tillandsia

Air plants need water, and do not, in fact, live on air. Like most plants, they require fair water, good light, and great air circulation. Humidity is not an adequate source of water.

You will need to water your plant. Not too much and not that often.

If you look at an air plant leaf, you will see the tiny grey suction scales (trichomes). These scales close up when the plant is well hydrated.

Air plants become dormant when left too long without water.

It is time for a water bath when the plant leaf is curled, wrinkled, lighter in colour, or not plump when touched. You can also mist the plants, but this can cause rot due to trapped water between the leaves.

Air plants are not fussy drinkers. You can use pond water or aquarium water, rain water, bottled water, or tap water, unless the tap water in your area is artificially softened and too high in sodium (salt).

Do not use distilled water because it is too pure and will draw nutrients out of the plant (this is true for all non-carnivorous plants).

It is best to soak your air plants in the morning because they soak up carbon dioxide from the air at night, and wet leaves will prevent them from "breathing."

Plan to soak your air plants once or twice a week, depending on how dry the air is in your environment. Let the plant soak for at least two hours, but preferably the entire day.

Generally, air plants do not require fertilizers. In fact, overfeeding the plants can cause more harm than good. A highly diluted bromeliad fertilizer is best if you really want to feed the plants.

After soaking, gently shake excess water from the plant and place it leaf-side down, allowing water trapped between the spiky leaves to drain. Let the plant sit for a few hours before designing.

Keep out of direct sunlight. You can tell how much light an air plant needs by the colour of its leaves. The puffier and firmer plants that are grey or even white, need more light, and the lighter green plants are more adapted for growing in the shade.

preserving flowers and foliage

how-to | select flowers to preserve

Pick your flowers just, just before they peak, and try to avoid harvesting flowers on a rainy day. Make sure each flower is completely dry.

how-to

make brittle, dried plant material pliant

Dried flowers and foliage become brittle over time, making them almost impossible to manipulate into a design without causing damage.

Spread lotion on all the leaves and set them down on a paper towel.

Within seconds the leaves will be pliable again, making them easier to work with.

how-to

steam dried flowers to reshape

Hold dried flowers or pods over steaming water to make them pliable. Reshape or repair any folds or dents.

how-to

clean dust from dried flowers with a blast of air

Blow away any dust on individual flowers or dried flower designs with your hairdryer set on low.

how-to | # turn baking soda into washing soda

Line an oven tray or casserole dish with baking/parchment paper.

Measure out 3/4 cup of the baking soda and sprinkle it evenly onto the oven tray.

Bake the baking soda in an oven at 200°C (390°F) for 30 minutes. This turns the baking soda (sodium bicarbonate) into washing soda (sodium carbonate).

Make sure you are extra careful when using washing soda. It is highly alkaline with a pH of 11, so wear protective gloves and glasses to avoid skin and eye irritation.

how-to | # make skeleton leaves

Choose a few leaves, keeping in mind that stronger, leathery leaves (such as magnolia) work best. Flip the leaf over and look at the veins. The more pronounced the vein network (venation) on the back of the leaf, the better the end result. Some leaves will discolour as their chlorophyll breaks down, while others (such as ivy) remain green.

Boil a full kettle of water and pour two cups into a saucepan over high heat. You will need the remaining water to top up your leafy soup as the water boils away. Dissolve the sodium carbonate. Add your leaves and turn the heat down to a simmer when the mixture starts to boil.

Gently simmer the leafy soup for 1.5 to 2 hours, topping up the water level as it evaporates.

When you notice the flesh becoming soft and floating away from the veins, lift the leaf out of the water with a spatula or the back of a large spoon and rinse in cold water.

Place the leaf on a smooth, flat surface and wipe off any creases with a brush. Blot away any moisture with a cotton bud.

Paint the leaf with water and start to brush away the fleshy pulp. Flip the leaf over and clean the other side.

When the skeleton leaf is dry, it will naturally pull away from the surface. Use a needle to carefully wiggle loose any bits that remain stuck.

how-to | # bleach skeleton leaves

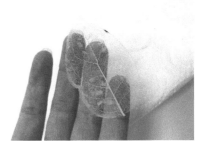

Place the leaves in a shallow dish and pour in enough bleach to just cover the leaves. The leaves will immediately start to bleach.

After a few minutes, the leaves will become a pale yellow and then a beautiful winter white.

how-to | skeleton-leaf bowl

Cover a container with cling wrap.

Pour wood glue into a bowl and thin it with some warm water. It should be the consistency of whipping cream.

Dip a skeleton leaf into the glue mixture.

Smooth the leaf onto the container by following the container's contours.

Keep adding glue-soaked leaves until the container is completely covered.

Smooth down the leaves, ensuring that each leaf adheres to the other leaves.

Set aside to dry completely.

Gently pull the cling wrap away from the container, and then even more gently remove the cling wrap from your skeleton-leaf bowl.

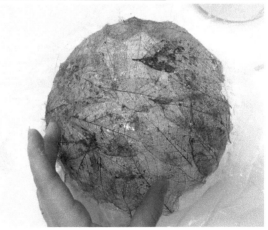

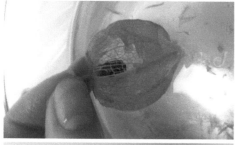
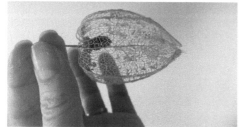

how-to | make skeleton physalis pods

Add a touch of fantasy to your design with the papery pods (sepals) covering the little berry of the Chinese Lantern plant. Fresh, the pods are gorgeous. Skeletonized, they add a luxurious lacy quality to your flowers.

Prepare the washing soda mixture as described for skeleton leaves.

Gently simmer the pods for 1.5 to 2 hours. Top up the water level as the water evaporates.

When you notice the flesh becoming soft and floating away from the veins, lift the pod out of the water. Rinse in cold water and set aside to dry.

You now have delicate skeletonized pods.

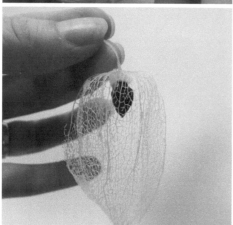

how-to | bleach skeleton physalis pods

Soak the pod in bleach.

Rinse in clean water.

how-to | # add wire stems and beads to the skeleton physalis pods

Press a thin wire into the opening of a bead, and secure with a drop of glue.

Snip the pod open to remove the dried berry and replace it with the bead on a wire.

Secure the bead to the pod with glue.

how-to | # air dry physalis pods

Cut the physalis stems and clean them by removing all foliage.

Tie the stems with a ribbon or string and hang them upside down in a well-ventilated area.

The papery pods (sepals) will retain their vivid colours, and the tiny fruit will shrivel and dry inside the pods.

how-to | make a twig wreath with beaded skeleton physalis pods

Cover the outside of the glass container with cling film. This makes it easy to remove the wreath and protects the glass from glue and scratches.

Lay your first twig on the glass container and glue a small bit of moss to the twig.

Glue a second twig to the first twig. Try to avoid gluing the twigs to the cling film. Add a small bit of moss.

Add another twig. Now you have a stable foundation to build the wreath up. It is important that each twig has at least three connection points. That means that every tiny twig should be attached to another twig in at least three places.

Add twigs all the way around the glass container. Try to remain true to the circular shape as much as possible.

Allow the glue to dry and then inspect it for stability by wiggling the twigs. Add more twigs where it is not completely stable, each time connecting them in at least three places.

Slip the wreath from the container and inspect the inside for any loose twigs. Again, add twigs where needed.

how-to | make skeleton hydrangeas

The how-to for skeletonizing hydrangeas is similar to that for leaves and pods described previously.

Snip away a few flowers (florets) from the mop head.

Boil the flowers in a water and washing soda soup.

Gently simmer the petal soup for 1.5 to 2 hours. Top up the water level as the water evaporates.

When you notice the flesh becoming soft and floating away from the veins, lift the hydrangea petals out of the water with a spatula or the back of a large spoon and rinse in cold water. Place the hydrangea petals on a smooth, flat surface and brush away any creases.

Paint the hydrangea petals with water and brush away the fleshy pulp.

how-to | # make skeleton blossoms from hydrangea petals

Start with the stamens by unraveling a section of sisal string.

Wrap a decorative wire around the sisal to tie it together. Let the wire extend to form the blossom's stem.

Cover the wire with florist tape where it is wrapped around the sisal. Extend longer for a decorative stem if required.

Fan out the sisal and dip the tips of the sisal in paint to create the anther.

Pin the stamens into polystyrene to make them stand upright while the paint dries.

Glue hydrangea petals to fan out around the stamens.

how-to | # dry hydrangeas naturally in water

Choose or harvest the flower heads in peak condition.

Set the stems in deep water, letting the heads rest on the sides of the vase for support.

Place the vase in a low light location to preserve as much of the natural colour as possible. Run your hand softly over the flowers—if they rustle like dried grass, they are ready to be used. The flowers will also be perfectly dry by the time the vase is empty.

how-to | # dry mushrooms for floral art

Let the mushrooms dry in a well-ventilated area. They will elegantly shrivel up and curl.

Store in a dry place.

how-to | # press flowers

Place plumper flowers between two sheets of paper towels to absorb moisture and prevent mildew. Position the flowers spaced out between the pages of an old magazine or heavy book and leave to dry. I have kept an old telephone book just for this. The weight of the book presses the flowers.

how-to | hang flowers to air-dry

Remove all foliage from the flower stem.

If you want to dry a bunch, make sure there is enough space between the stems for air to circulate.

Hang the stems upside down in a low-lit, well-ventilated space.

how-to | dry flowers in the microwave

Flowers with lower water content, such as hydrangeas, dry beautifully and within minutes in the microwave.

Snip the individual flowers from the hydrangea mop head.

Place the florets between a few layers of paper towel. Place it in a saucer and microwave for 30 seconds, on the lowest setting.

Turn the flowers and microwave again for 30 seconds. Keep checking the flowers to make sure the moisture in the stems does not boil. Mine took about 2 minutes in one microwave and 3 minutes in another.

Experiment by starting with the lowest setting for only 30 seconds at a time. Different settings will also produce different colour variations.

how-to | dry flowers in silica gel

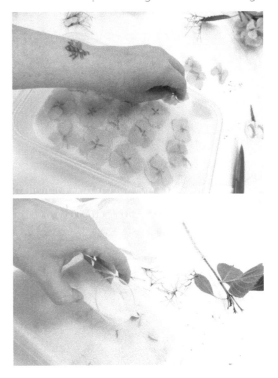

Silica gel draws out all moisture from the flowers and preserves them perfectly. This could take up to a week.

Pour a thin layer of crystals in an airtight container. Snip the flowers and place them on the silica gel.

Cover the flowers with another layer of silica gel. Close the container, making sure it is completely airtight.

Flowers dried in silica gel must be protected from water. The gel weakens the flowers, and it becomes mushy when wet. Do not bleach flowers dried in silica gel because the blooms simply dissolve.

how-to | dry flowers in glycerine

Flowers remain more pliable when dried in glycerine.

Place the stems in a solution of 50% water and 50% glycerine.

Set aside to dry completely in a low light area.

how-to | know when the flowers are dry

Run your fingers lightly over the flowers. If they rustle like grass, they are perfectly dry, and should remain colour-fast for years.

how-to | design a dried hydrangea grass-fountain

Tie bundles of grass with elastic bands.

Cut the blades of grass to a blunt and equal length, just below the elastic band.

Place a Kenzan in a shallow container (see later in the book for more detailed instructions on how to use a Kenzan).

Place the grass bundles by inserting them into the metal nails of the Kenzan to fountain out.

Conceal the Kenzan and elastic bands by adding frosted glass pebbles to the container.

Add water to keep the grass hydrated.

Glue in dried hydrangeas with flower glue.

hydration and staying put

*"welcome, loved, and comfortable...
and now we offer the flower a drink of water
and somewhere nice to sit."*

The previous chapter explained how to minimize trauma and how to condition our carefully selected flowers. It only makes sense now to pay attention to how we can enjoy their beauty for as long as possible.

I rarely, if ever, design dry. I even have a trick for a secret water source for wired body flowers. (see page 303)

This is a great opportunity for innovation because every design requires a unique solution to keep those flowers in place and hydrated.

First, I look at floral foam—what it is, how to use it, and the reasons why contemporary designers search for (new and old) alternatives to display and design our flowers in.

The vases, containers, and other hollow alternatives we select to design in greatly influence the personality of our arrangements. I look at glass, metal, pottery (including unbaked clay and paper), and baskets and ways to support and style flowers in these various materials to match a creative vision.

I then move on to crafting armatures, using water tubes as a water source, and placing stems in these tubes so that they remain hydrated for as long as possible.

I end the chapter with a few creative design ideas to spark the imagination.

floral foam

It is impossible to discuss hydration of cut flowers in designs without at least mentioning floral foam, even though I rarely, if ever, design with it.

Floral foam is an open-celled phenolic foam that easily soaks up water and can be used as a base for flower arrangements.

Designers who are environmentally aware shy away from using foam because it is made of phenol formaldehyde resin, which can only be used once as a water source and is either not biodegradable at all or will biodegrade by 51.5% in a year in biologically active landfill conditions.

But sometimes using floral foam is the only logical mechanic for a design. In these situations it is best to design with the full life cycle of your art in mind. Have a creative plan for repurposing the used foam (or plastic lining or wax barrier) other than it becoming trash. Taking responsibility for your designs once they fade should always be part of your design philosophy.

how-to | soak floral foam

Mix flower food with water.

Float the block on top of the water. Do not dunk it because dunking traps air bubbles inside the foam.

how-to | # choose the right foam for your design

There are three types of floral foam:

- Dry foam used for artificial flowers or dried flowers (usually a grey block).

- Wet foam used for fresh-cut flower designs (usually a green block).

- And coloured foam, which is similar to wet foam but has a higher density and comes in a variety of colours. Rainbow Foam is the trademarked name for the coloured floral foam produced by Smithers-Oasis.

Floral foam is available in different pre-cut shapes and sizes, and is easy to carve and shape with a sharp, long-blade knife.

how-to | # know when the floral foam is soaked

Each block of foam holds 40 times its own weight in water.

One brick holds 2 liters of water. When the block sinks, it's ready to use.

The Rainbow Oasis has a stronger density than ordinary wet foam and will float below the surface when fully saturated.

how-to | # carve floral foam shapes

Roughly cut the desired shape out of floral foam, using a sharp knife with a long blade. For my design, I cut pebbles out of foam.

Final shaping of floral foam is best done with another piece of foam. Use it like you would sandpaper.

Sand the pebble to a smooth finish.

Soak the shape as described previously if you are using it as a water source.

how-to | # seal floral foam shapes with candle wax to make them watertight

Dip the flat bottom of the un-soaked floral foam pebble in melted candle wax.

Rest the pebbles, wax-side up, allowing the wax to set. The wax will become hard, forming a watertight layer at the bottom. You can now soak the pebbles as normal.

how-to | # conceal floral foam

Floral foam, except for coloured foam, should be covered in some way so that your mechanics are not visible. Wrap the foam in foliage, or use flowers, moss, sisal, or another decorative method.

You can conceal the foam before designing, conceal it with your design, or add bits afterward to only cover certain areas.

View your design from all sides to make sure the mechanics are concealed.

how-to | # insert stems into floral foam

Wet floral foam crumbles easily, and stems (especially heavy stems) will destroy the foam as you insert them.

If you want to re-insert a stem, do so at a slightly different position, and do not simply press the stem back into the same hole. This way you ensure that your stems have access to water.

Make a wire cage to protect the shape of wet foam in larger designs.

how-to | # insert a dried flower stem into wet floral foam

Keep the dried flower stem (or in this case, a dried mushroom) from getting wet and spoiling by inserting the stem into a drinking straw before placing it in the wet foam. The plastic straw creates a moisture barrier.

Use a clear straw so that it completely disappears in your design.

how-to | # insert a fresh floral stem into dry floral foam

Keep the fresh flower stem hydrated by placing it in its own secret water source. Cut a drinking straw to the required size. Seal a drinking straw with hot glue on one end and fill it with water. Insert the flower into the drinking straw so that the stem is in water. Design with the drinking straw as you would with the stem. This way it is easy to top up the water.

how-to | # line containers

Protect containers from rust or water damage by lining it with thick plastic before adding the floral foam. Cut away any plastic that might show in your design.

Paper, terra-cotta, and other unbaked clay containers should also be lined to prevent damage.

Any item that may not be watertight, such as hollowed-out fruit, vegetables, pods, or even books, should be lined.

When in doubt, line the container with plastic.

how-to | # top up water

Top up water regularly because arrangements designed in floral foam fade faster than those in water. As little as 10% moisture loss will cause wilting because floral foam pulls water from the flowers when it dries.

Wet floral foam can be topped up by pouring water into the container. Rainbow Oasis floral foam needs to be topped up by pouring water onto the foam where the stems are inserted into the foam.

how-to | # keep soaked floral foam

Floral foam that dried after previously being soaked will not take up sufficient water with a second soaking. It is therefore best to keep large chunks of unused, soaked floral foam in a plastic bag with water so that it remains moist for later use.

If you must re-soak floral foam, try soaking it in really warm water and always cut the foam to see if it is fully saturated.

how-to | # discard used floral foam

Floral foam is not compostable. Used foam can only become trash, so do not discard it in your compost heap, garbage disposal, or drain.

Do not use the floral foam block more than once.

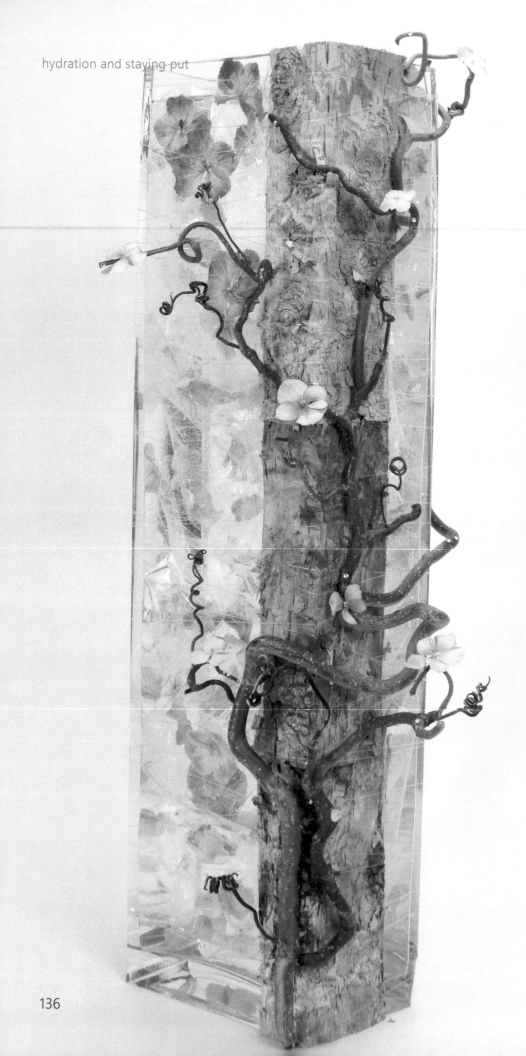

vases, containers, and hollow alternatives

The container greatly influences the design. The shape, size, colour, texture, and material of the container will guide your flower choice and on which mechanics you will use to support the flowers in the design.

The goal is for the flowers and the container to form a unit, as an extension of each other. The flowers and the container should not compete.

The personality of a vase sets the tone. Glass containers are the most versatile and can adapt to the environment. Shiny containers are usually more formal, and a rustic, clay jug would be more informal.

Make sure the container does not grab the attention nor overwhelm the overall design. I am from the school of thought that flowers should always be your focal point and tell the story.

Follow the shape of the vase when designing.

There are obviously exceptions to this rule, but in most cases your design needs to be 1.5 to 2 times the height of the vase.

how-to | # design outside in

Cover the container, either completely or in part, with bark, foliage, or, well, anything that suits your creative vision.

You can wrap it with decorative wire, almost invisible fishing line, or glue or tape details to the outside of the container.

Covering is a fast and inexpensive way to transform ugly containers, give overused containers a new look, hide a chip or flaw, or create a unit out of mismatched pieces.

Of course, you can use this technique to add another decorative element to the container you are already designing with.

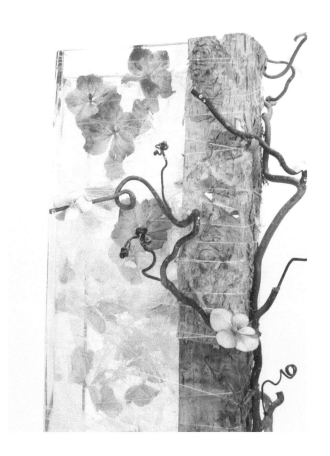

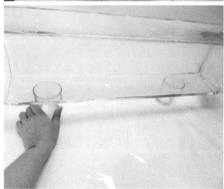
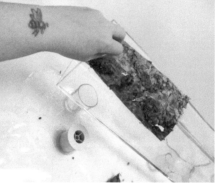

how-to | # wrap the outside of a container

Measure out the bark.

Score the bark to create a cutting line.

Cut the bark to size, and soak for a few hours in warm water.

Fold the strip of bark so that it follows the container's curves. Secure the bark to the container by wrapping it tightly with fishing line.

Overlap pieces of bark to create a continuous effect.

how-to | submerge flowers with cellophane

Snip the individual florets from the hydrangea mop head.

Drop a few flowers into the vase.

Scrunch up some clear cellophane and place it over the flowers. Gently push the cellophane into place with a long dowel.

Continue to add layers of hydrangeas and cellophane.

Fill the vase with water.

Add decorative elements. I used dried hydrangeas on the outside of the vase to contrast with the submerged hydrangeas on the inside of the vase.

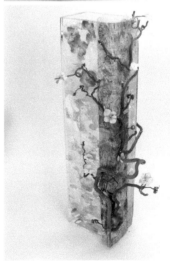

glass

🌿 Generally, there is no need to line glass vases and containers. Obvious exceptions are if you want to conceal mechanics or if you are protecting the glass from scratches or rust.

🌿 Make sure the water is always clear, without bits of floating plant material.

🌿 Cold water will naturally show some bubbles if left to stand. For more deliberate bubbles, use carbonated water.

🌿 Lime buildup on glass containers can be cleaned by filling the container with water and dissolving a denture cleaning tablet in it.

🌿 You can colour the water with food-colouring. This will change the colour of the flowers as well because the flower soaks up the pigments.

how-to | # submerged design

Flowers deteriorate faster when designed under water.

Add a few drops of bleach to the water to keep it clear.

Position the flowers carefully in the bottom of a clean, empty glass container, taking care not to bruise them.

Place some wire, curled up twigs, or crumpled up cellophane over the flowers to keep them in place, and add another layer of flowers.

Add enough of the layering material, in this case willow stems, to weigh the flowers down and prevent them from floating up once you add water.

Fill the container with water after positioning all your flowers.

The flowers will rise, shift, and reposition themselves, so allow for some spontaneity.

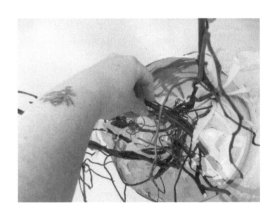

metal

🌿 Line metal containers to protect them from rust.

🌿 Metal tends to neutralize flower food in the water. You can avoid this by placing another container (glass, plastic, or pottery) inside the metal container.

how-to | # prevent rust on metal containers

Paint the bottom edge of the can with clear nail varnish, or any varnish, to keep it from rusting

pottery

✿ Baked clay or pottery containers are almost as convenient and hassle-free to design in as glass. They tend to have a more distinct personality than glass and are therefore less versatile, but they are not clear, so it is easier to hide mechanics.

✿ Unbaked, terra-cotta, precious china, and paper pulp containers should always be lined or protected with another container inside it or with varnish.

how-to | make a bamboo peg

Hana-Kubari is an Ikebana flower mechanic.

Cut three sections of fresh bamboo and carefully split the bamboo lengthwise. It is easier to split the bamboo in the inter-node rather than on the node.

Slip the bamboo over the container's edge.

Gently push the bamboo down to split it open, taking care not to split the entire stem in two.

Tilt the bamboo stems to the side, creating a gap for the flower stem.

Fill the containers with water.

Slip in the stem to catch between the bamboo and the container. It should fit in snugly enough to stay in place but not pinched so that the flowering stem can still take up water.

baskets

🌿 Baskets should be lined or have another lightweight container placed inside to hold the design.

🌿 Make sure the container or lining inside the basket doesn't distract from the overall look of the design.

how-to | make a hanging wreath basket

Cut a dried wreath into sections and choose a perfect circle to build the basket on.

Wire in a few stems to follow the shape at the handle, and then two stems that split open at the bottom to create the basket.

Cut snippets of twigs and glue them to follow the shape at the handle. Fill in the gaps at the basket end.

Glue in tendrils.

Place the orchid plant in a sisal mat, and wire to secure. Glue a few twigs to the sisal to make it blend in with the basket.

support

Flowers need some kind of support to keep them in place in your design, whether the stems are placed to stand in a wadded-up ball of wire tightly wedged into your container, or in a heavy flower frog (made from glass, lead, or pottery) that sits in the bottom of your container, or in something that somehow suspend the flowers over your container.

  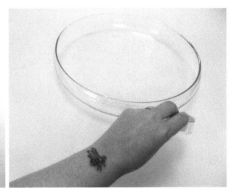

how-to | tape a grid

Taping a grid over the top of a container creates space for flowers to rest on so that they can stand in the water exactly where you place the stem.

Secure all the pieces of tape by taping around the outside of the vase, neatly finishing off the grid.

how-to | ...tape a grid, sticky side out

I usually turn the tape sticky side out, so that I can secure floral details on the tape and still have the benefit of a grid to rest my flowers on.

how-to | rethink komiwara

Komiwara is a classic and traditional Ikebana technique used in Rikka designs. Designers would usually bundle straw to keep the flowers in place.

Set the container on its side to make it easier to pack.

Add a handful of reeds and bamboo pieces.

I used larger bamboo pieces as temporary spacers for where the poppy-seed heads will be placed.

I packed 3/4 of the container to allow the reeds to rest at an angle. You can also fill it completely for a more upright look.

Hold the bamboo in place with your hand and right the container.

Slowly let the bamboo pieces settle by twisting the vase to create a spiral.

Remove the bamboo spacers and place the poppy-seed heads.

Fill the container with water and add the clematis tendrils.

hydration and staying put

how-to | # permanently fix with clay, concrete, or play dough

Balance is all important, especially when designing with a stick-tree. The design mechanics (a stick-tree in this example) must be solid, stable, and well balanced even before you start designing.

Place a few twigs, sticks, and a thicker branch (or two) in a plastic container to create a decorative tree.

Secure them in place with clay, concrete, or play dough.

Allow to dry.

Remove it from the plastic container or set it in another container.

Add the design elements and floral details.

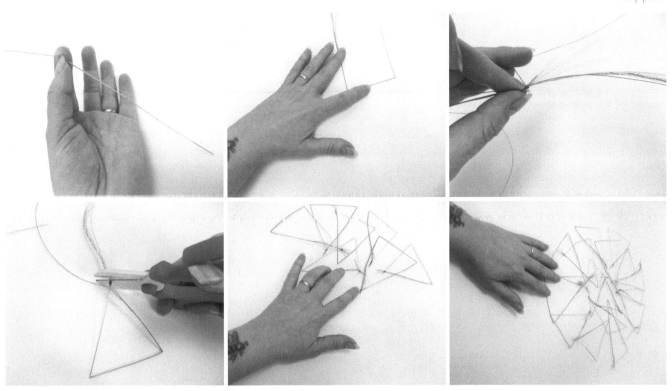

how-to | bend grass into triangles for a barely there spiderweb

Pinch the delicate blade of grass lightly between your nail and the pad of your finger. These techniques are explained in more detail later in the book.

Do not break the grass. Gently bend it into shape.

Secure the triangle by wrapping another blade of grass around it, ending with a knot. Place the triangles on a flat working surface. Design and glue the spiderweb pattern.

Add water tubes for your floral details.

how-to | weave a vase stopper tube

Measure the inside diameter of the vase.

Make circles of that diameter using the stronger part of blades of grass (the pieces closest to the roots) and secure with glue.

The circles should fit snugly into the vase.

Weave the circles into long blades of grass to create a tube. Weaving techniques are explained in more detail later in the book.

Wiggle the woven part into the vase.

Fill with sufficient water to cover the stem ends of the long blades of grass to keep them hydrated.

Keep the flowers in place by slipping the stems through the woven grass with the stems inside, in the water.

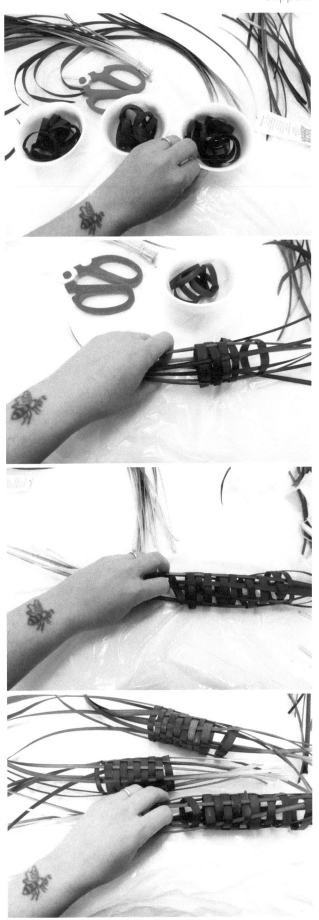

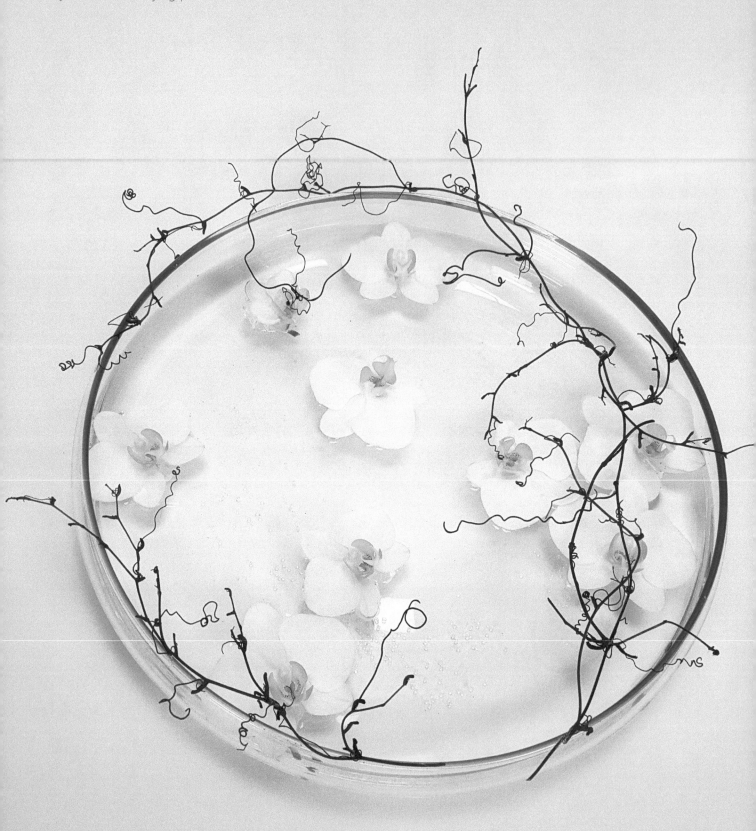

how-to | cut a bubble raft to float flowers

Flowers float in water. They just don't always naturally float on water. They sometimes need a bit of help.

Water slowly seeps in between the petals to pool and weigh down the bloom.

Cut a bubble wrap raft to fit like a skirt around the flower base.

Cut a disk of bubble wrap just slightly smaller than the flower's petals.

The heavier the flower head, the larger the bubble wrap raft. The bubble raft will be almost invisible in water.

Fold the wrap in quarters and cut a hole for the stem to fit through.

Simply slip the stem through the hole.

Cut the stem as short as desired and set it in the water to float.

Even flat-petaled orchids float better with a bubble raft.

how-to | wire tangle support

Loosely scrunch up wire in a ball and place in a container. The ball should fit snugly and firmly against the sides of the container.

Fill the container with water and simply slip flowers through the wire to set them in place.

For this design, I exaggerated the technique a bit and extended the wire to form a swirl over the top of the container. To cover the swirl, slide blades of grass through the wire so that the stem ends are in water. Randomly interweave the grass through the wire swirl. Insert the gerbera stem through the wire and grass swirl to keep it hydrated.

how-to | use moss as a support

Soak a ball of moss in water.

Poke a hole in the moss with a bamboo skewer where you want to add the stems.

You can use similar methods to place and support stems, as you do when using a Kenzan.

Thicker stems need to be cut sharp into a spear, so that they can be inserted into the moss.

how-to | # use a kenzan

A Kenzan is a pin holder to hold plant material in place. It was invented for Moribana, an Ikebana style of arrangement with *Moru* meaning heaped, and *Hana* meaning flowers. A Kenzan is usually made from metal or plastic embedded in a metal base.

Knead a small ball of floral fix to make it sticky and pliable.

Roll the floral fix into a snake and connect the two ends.

Turn the Kenzan, pin-side down, and place the floral fix on the flat side.

Press the Kenzan down, pin-side up, in the design container.

Grasp the Kenzan firmly and, while pressing down, start to twist.

The doughnut-shaped floral fix will allow air to escape as you press and twist, creating a vacuum between the container and the Kenzan.

The vacuum bond is secure and stable, and will not come loose from the container.

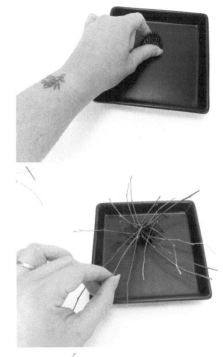

how-to | # support a weak stem with a wire

Weak but tall-stemmed flowers cannot support themselves in a Kenzan. Give them extra support by pressing a wire into the spongy inside of soft stems.

how-to | # bundle up

Gather a few blades of grass together and secure. It is easier to press into the nails of a Kenzan as a bundle. You can always trim the bundle if you need less grass in the design.

how-to | # prevent heavier stems from toppling over

Place a rock or heavy object on the Kenzan to weigh it down so that it does not topple over.

how-to | # add support for hollow stems

Press a sturdy stem into the hollow inside of the stem to give it extra support.

how-to | # prevent spongy stems from splitting and curling

Some stems (like calla lilies) curl up when placed in water. Wrap florist tape around spongy stems to prevent them from splitting or curling in the Kenzan.

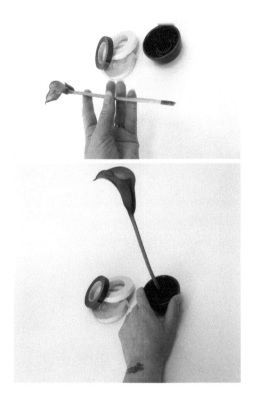

how-to | # make your own kenzan

Pour candle wax in a shallow container (I used a canning jar lid) and press wires into the wax. Weigh the wax Kenzan down with pebbles or glass beads to prevent it from floating in the water.

You can make a heavier Kenzan by hammering sharp nails through wood, or gluing them into a stone, pebble, tile, or brick. You will have to drill holes into these, or simply cast nails into cement, as you would with the wax.

how-to | cross-cut a heavier branch

Cut through a branch, turn the branch and cut again to quarter it. This makes it easier to press into the nails of a Kenzan. This is also the best way to adjust the branch's position.

how-to | position stems at an angle

Place a thin twig in the position you want to angle the flower and slip the soft stem over the twig to stand in the exact position desired.

how-to | # clean the kenzan

Use a cuticle pusher or wooden skewer to clean out any debris between the Kenzan nails.

how-to | # brush-clean the kenzan

Make a brush out of the hard end (closest to the roots) of a flax leaf (the part you usually cut away between the stem and the ripped pieces) and sweep up any tiny fibers left on the Kenzan.

how-to | # catch bits of plant material

Place a net, or old stocking, over the Kenzan before you start. Then simply lift the net and debris away when done. This is especially useful when you use a Kenzan to rip foliage.

how-to | # use the double vase trick

Craft a dry layer of glass by placing a smaller vase inside the larger vase, creating a double layer.

Vases of any shape can be used to create a glass layered design.

Fill the outer layer with water and position the flowers in the gaps.

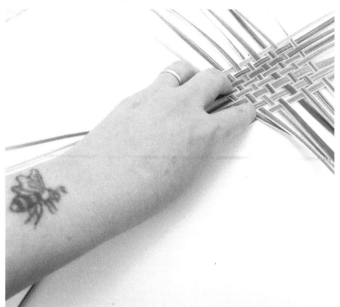

weave a grass dome

Weave a carpet of grass and rest it on the container.

Wiggle the grass weave open, allowing it to bulge into a dome.

how-to | # use the double vase trick in a few more ways

You can, of course, create more than just two layers by slipping multiple vases into the stack.

Place a candle in the center and flowers in the outer layer.

Fragile skeleton leaves can be pressed securely to the sides of an outer layer and fresh flowers added in a water-filled inner layer.

Place playing cards, blocks, fruit, or a special note in the outer layer. Whatever creativity inspires in you.

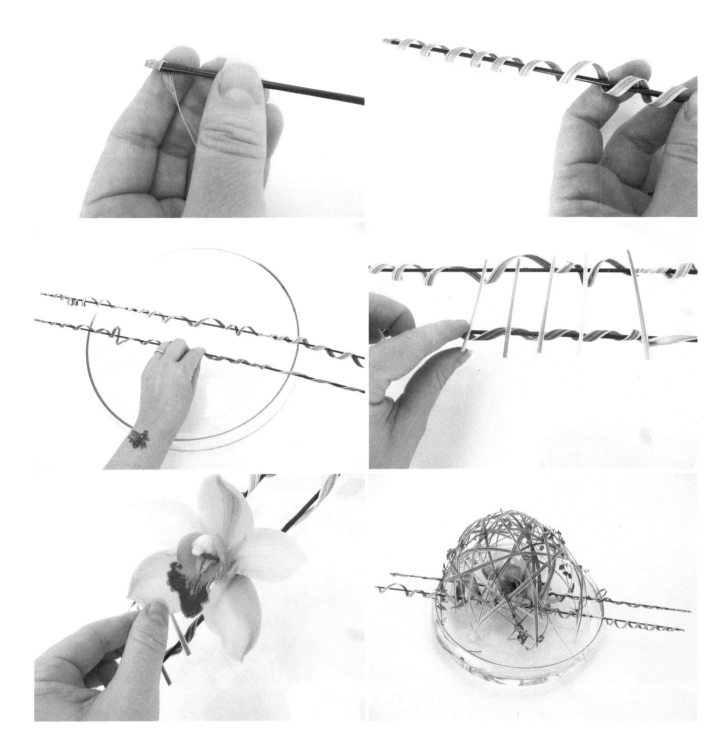

how-to | suspend flowers above water with two wires

Wrap two wires with blades of grass.

Add a few connecting pieces of grass for the flowers to rest on, suspending them above the water with their stems in the water.

armatures and water sources

A floral design can be classified as either a construction or a structure, depending on whether the water source for fresh plant material is hanging in the design or if the design is standing in water. Which is which depends greatly on who you ask, so I prefer the old-fashioned term *armatures* as a blanket statement. But mostly, I like the idea of such an old-fashioned term describing my contemporary design style, so I go with that.

Armatures can range from the uncomplicated to the elaborate, and everything in-between. The possibilities are absolutely endless. You can use armatures to stretch your design budget by creating a large display with relatively inexpensive floral ingredients, or turn a single focal flower into an event all of its own.

Armature designs will test your skills, from how to tie knots to how to balance heavily laden branches.

Great armatures are part of the foundation of extraordinary designs. Don't try to build something spectacular on a shaky foundation. Nothing is more frustrating or more time consuming than trying to make do with something that is seconds away from falling apart, or working around mechanics that are not sturdy or well thought through.

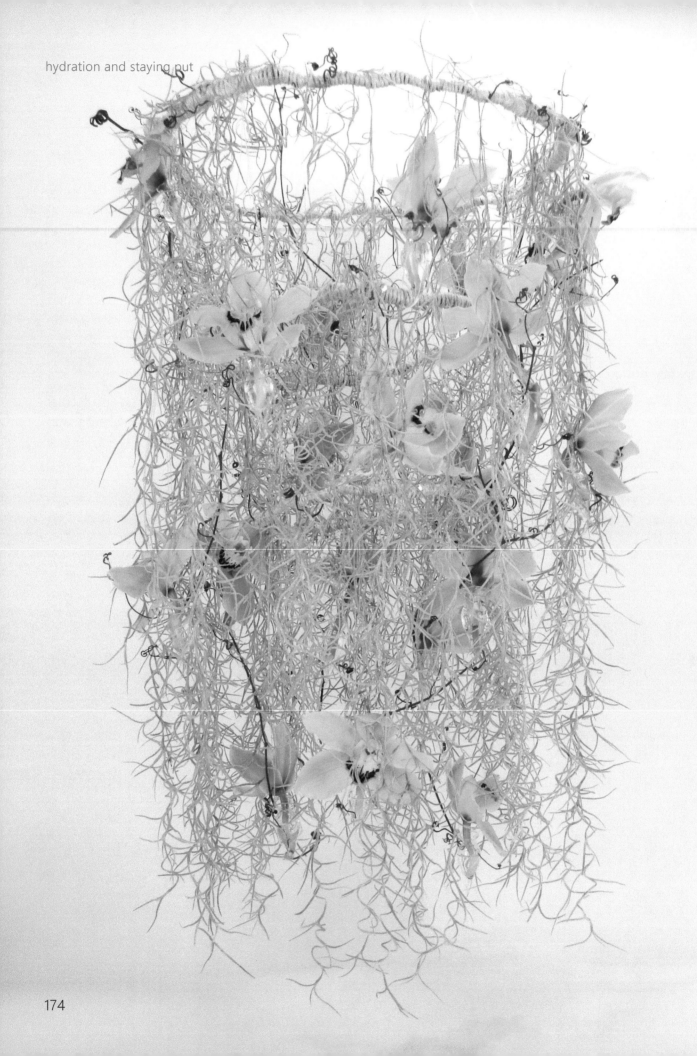

attaching a water source

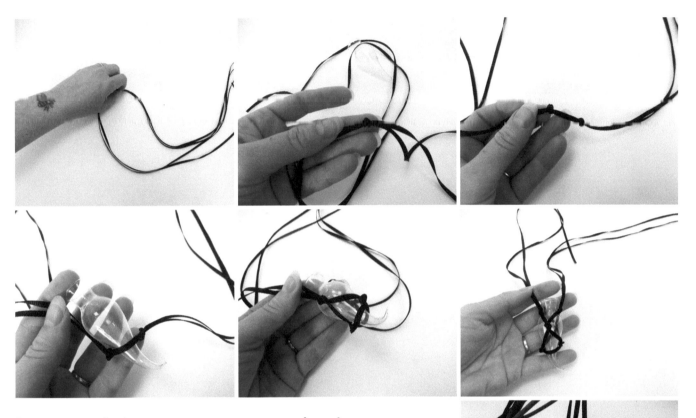

how-to | # hang macramé glass sea horses

I used fishing line to hang the tubes in this design, but I will illustrate the technique with ribbon because it is easier to see.

Cut two long lengths of ribbon for each glass bubble you want to hang. Find the midpoint by folding the ribbon in half. Open the fold and knot the ribbon 1 cm (1/2 in) from the midpoint on each side to create a catch for the glass bubble.

Use opposite ends of the ribbon to make a knot 2.5 cm (1 in) above the first. Do the same on the other side.

Slip a glass bubble into the ribbon catch.

Again, use opposite ends of the ribbon to knot tightly on each side around the bubble's neck. It should look like a corset.

Hang the bubbles from the ribbon or line.

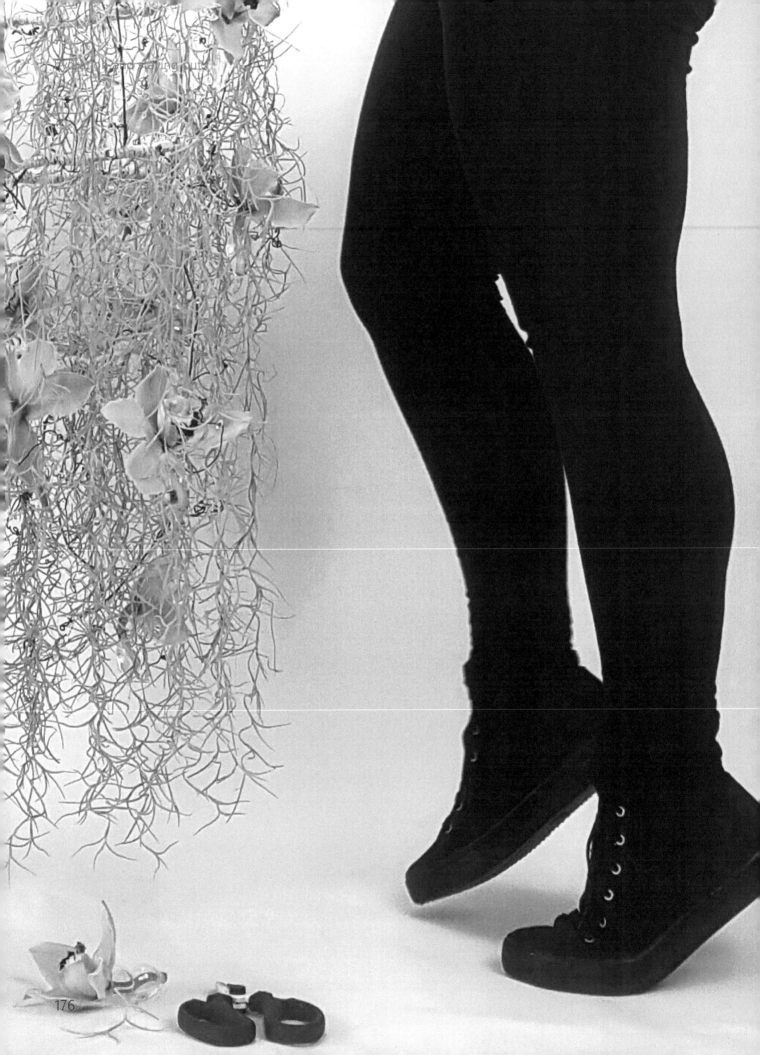

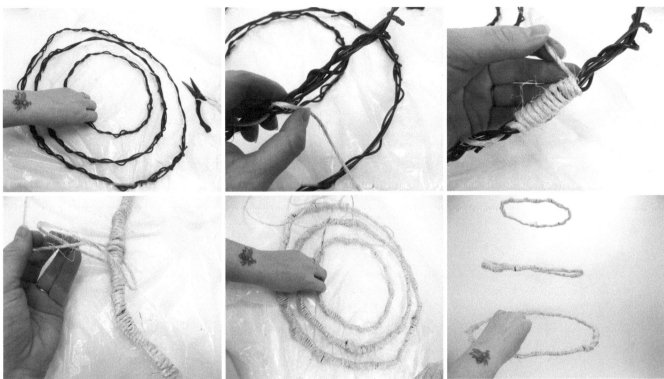

how-to | three tier chandelier

Bend and weave three wire wreaths.

Catch the end of a length of sisal through an opening in the wire wreath and secure it.

Wrap the sisal around the wire wreath, knotting the end to secure it.

Wrap the other two wreaths with sisal.

String up and hang the wreaths by connecting them with fishing line. String them—large to small for a chandelier, or small to large for a Christmas tree look.

Your design will twirl if you hang it by gathering and knotting all the lines at the top in a single knot. You can create a static design by hanging it from at least three points.

Place the orchids in glass vases and hang them from the wreaths.

Drape Spanish moss down the design.

how-to | # twig fork

Suspend the water tube in a fork of a stem. This is great if you want the flowers to hang horizontally or sink into a design.

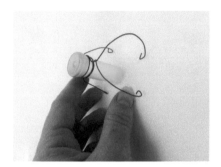

how-to | # spider legs

Wrap two wires around the water tube and curl them into legs so that the water tube is kept upright.

how-to | # over the side

Turn a twig upside down and use a fork in the twig as a hook to hang your water tube.

how-to | # butterfly feelers

Wrap wire twice around the tube and twist to secure. Curl the wire ends into butterfly feelers, making it easy to hang in a design. This is great if you want to allow the flowers to swing and move in the design.

how-to | wire handles

Place a wire over the mouth of the jar and fold it down the jar's sides.

Wrap another wire around the throat of the jar and twist the ends, securing the first wire.

Pull the first wire up to create a handle and curl its ends to catch around the second wire.

Hang the jars in your design.

how-to | ... on a stick

Toward the end of this chapter I show you how I make my own drinking straw water tubes. It is easy to modify those by gluing a stem into the bottom. You can also wire stems to water tubes.

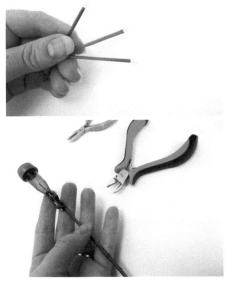

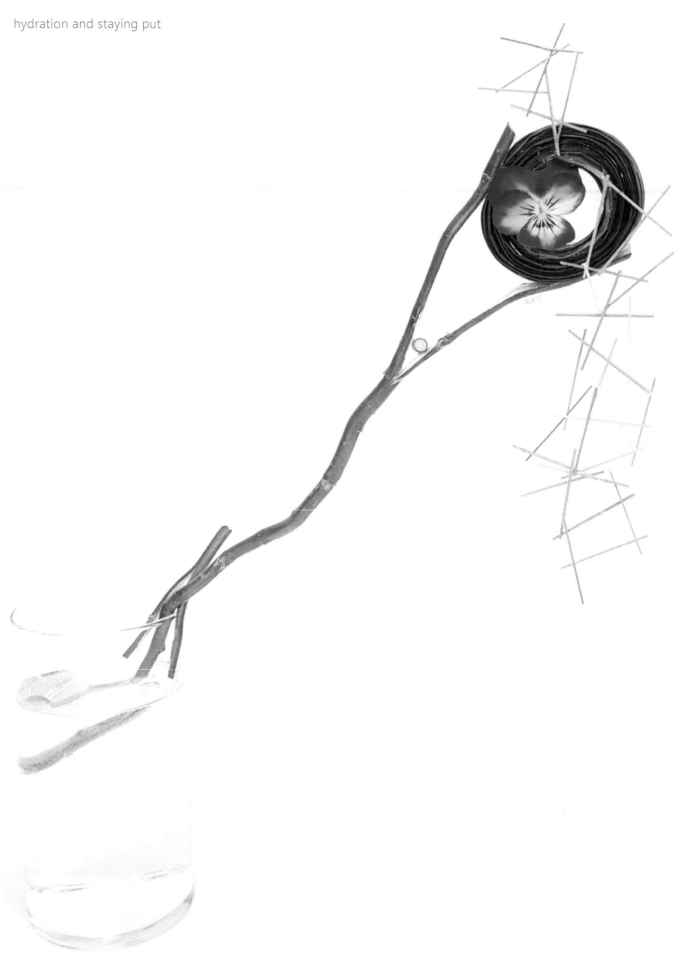

how-to | # glue

Glue a water tube to the back of your design with a tiny drop of hot glue.

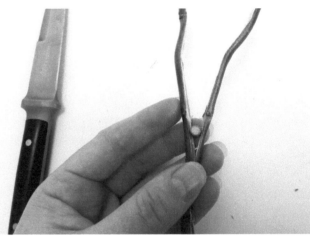

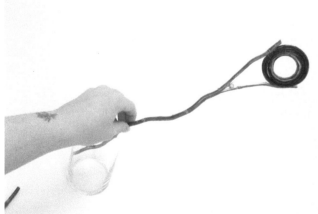

how-to | # peg and pinch

Split a fresh willow stem with a sharp knife.

Open the stem up and place a spacer stem to keep the split open.

Slip the lily grass reel into the split to pinch it in place. Secure it with a few tiny drops of floral glue if needed.

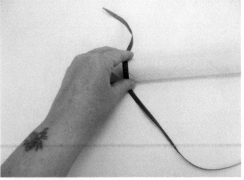

how-to | # grass reel

Measure the width of the blade of lily grass against a cardboard roll.

Cut a ring from the roll of the exact width of the grass. Wrap the paper roll ring with green florist tape.

Wind lily grass around the outside, and inside, of the cardboard ring.

how-to | # scattered grass garland

Snip a few blades of grass into tiny sections.

Glue the snippets one at a time into a pattern.

Secure each grass snippet in at least three places to another grass snippet.

Add a few random snippets to break the pattern.

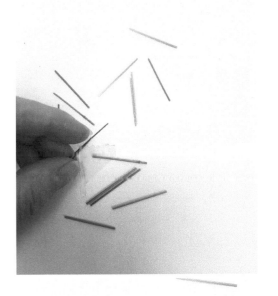

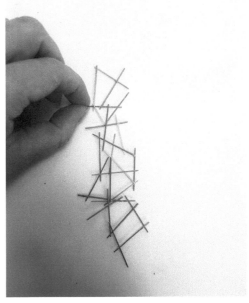

filling water tubes

- Any kind of pipette will make the job easier.

- I make two versions. The small and medium ones are syringe-and-tube versions for small containers, and the larger one is an upcycled soda bottle version, for filling many containers in a short amount of time.

- The tube has the added benefit of being flexible, so it is easier to get into awkward spots and refill those tiny tubes without disturbing floral details.

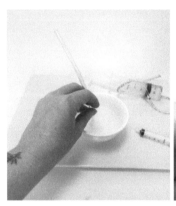   

how-to | syringe and tube

Heat the tube slightly with warm water and slide onto the syringe.

how-to | soda bottle pipette

It is not always possible to pack absolutely everything you might need, especially when traveling for competitions. You might not know where to find a large pipette in an unfamiliar country, or have time to search for one, but you will always find a soda or water bottle.

Remove the label and rinse the bottle thoroughly.

Cut or drill a small hole in the cap. Fit a pipe through the hole and secure with silicone glue.

The cap and tube take almost no packing space, and all you have to do is find a bottle on arrival.

how-to | # suck water from a container

Water can be sucked out of a heavy or overfull container with the syringe tube.

This is also a precise way to adjust water levels if you want an exact amount in multiple vases.

how-to | # suck water from water tubes

Suck water from tubes with a syringe tube after overfilling or before dismantling your design.

how-to | # wash water tubes

After every use, wash the water tubes in soapy warm water and rinse thoroughly to prevent the spread of bacteria. Add a bit of bleach to the soapy water if the tubes have held water for a while and they turned murky.

how-to | # dry water tubes

Drill a few holes into a wooden block and add wooden skewers to support the water tubes while they dry.

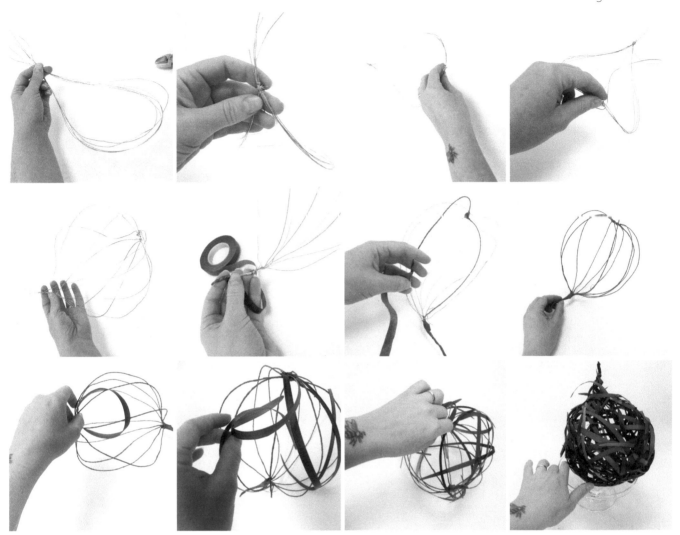

how-to | interweave a grass cocoon

Cut wires and bend them in half to form teardrop shapes.

Secure them at both ends.

Bend the wires open to shape the cocoon and wrap each wire in florist tape.

Set the wire flat on a working surface to see where it naturally rests, so that you can design accordingly.

Interweave blades of grass to create the cocoon shape.

placing flower stems

how-to | protect the stem

Wrap a band of florist tape around the stem before you wire it to hang.

Be careful not to cut or bruise the flower with rough handling. The wire should be tight enough to hold the stem, but not so tight that it forms a tourniquet that will strangle the stem and prevent it from taking up water, or even weaken it to the point of snapping.

how-to | hang flower stems, right side up

By right-side up, I mean the flowers are pointing up.

Fill the water tube with water. Insert the stem as far down as it can go. The flower will now be able to drink until the water tube is empty.

how-to | hang flower stems, upside down

Do not press the stems all the way in when hanging the flower upside down. The stem end should be closer to the seal. This way the stem will remain exposed to water for as long as possible.

how-to | # place thicker stems into water tubes with lids

Make sure the hole in the lid is not too tight for the stem because it can form a tourniquet, squeezing the stem so tight that it can't take up water.

Rather, cut a small slit in the plastic lid to make sure the stem slips through the hole without being constricted or compressed.

how-to | # seal any leaks

Petroleum jelly is waterproof and is not water soluble, so it creates a strong barrier to keep water from leaking out of the vials when you hang it upside down. In fact, this trick works so well that you can use drinking straws or plastic tubes, and simply seal around the stem with petroleum jelly.

how-to | # top up upside-down hanging water tubes

Snip away the flat bottom of the plastic tube to make it easy to top up water with a pipette or syringe tube.

how-to | # orchids

Orchid flowers should be cut from the plant by cutting the plant stem, and not just the flower stem, because they take up water better through the green stem and will last considerably longer.

This changes the position of stem placement and is not always possible, but it does make a difference.

concealing water tubes

🌿 Only conceal water tubes if it improves the overall look of your design, because sometimes trying to conceal a water tube actually draws more attention to it.

🌿 You can design with glass tubes as-is, without concealing them.

🌿 Inexpensive plastic water tubes look better concealed.

🌿 I often use my tiny drinking straw water tubes as-is. They are so small that they completely disappear in the overall design.

how-to | # petal or leaf cover

Place double-sided tape (or sticky-side-out clear tape) around the water tube. Smooth down the petals over the tube.

Make sure to overlap the petals so that the tube is still concealed when the petals start to dry.

how-to | # place the water tube in a hollow stem

Simply slip a water tube into a hollow stem, bamboo, or hollowed-out wood.

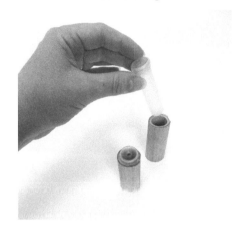

how-to | # wrap a stem around a water tube

Start at the bottom of the water tube and overlap the stem end.

Wind the weaving stem around the tube to just before the seal.

Knot the stem on itself.

how-to | # cover the water tube with bark

Soak the bark in warm water to make it pliable, then wrap it around the water tube.

Secure with wire or fishing line for an almost invisible look.

how-to | wrap a water tube with ribbon

Place a small, sticky-dot, clear tape, or double-sided tape on the bottom of the tube. Stick the tip of the tape to the tube and tape it sticky-side out over the tip of the test tube. Smooth the tape flat over the water tube.

Have a look at your ribbon to see if it has a "right side." Some ribbons are matte on one side and shiny on the other. Place the side you like best face-down and stick to the tube.

Measure the ribbon. The short leg of the ribbon should be at least twice the length of the test tube.

Smooth the ribbon flat over the upside-down clear tape to secure.

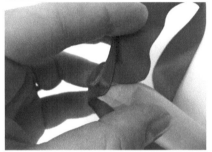

Fold the long end of the ribbon at a 90-degree angle. The right side of the ribbon will now cover the rest of the test tube.

Wrap the ribbon around the test tube, covering the entire sticky area. Spiral wrap the ribbon all the way to the top and tie the two ribbon ends in a tight knot.

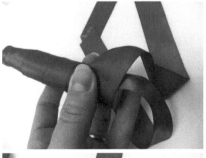

I like to leave the top seal of the test tube to show at the back. This way the recipient can see that the stem is in water. Also, this makes it easier to open the seal to top up the water, without having to undo the ribbon.

creative hydration solutions

drinking straw water tubes

Make your own tiny water tubes for when you want to add a tiny stem into a tiny space. It is especially suitable for orchids, because they are slow drinkers with thin stems. One tiny tube can keep a single orchid hydrated for days and can easily be topped up.

Not all drinking straws are created equal. There are fat ones and thin ones. Strong ones and flimsy ones. By now, I am a bit of a drinking straw collector. I know exactly where I can find the fatter straws or coloured straws. And yes, I always take my straws home with me. Upcycling in action, I think.

Cut the straws to size and seal the opening with a drop of hot glue.

Carefully inspect each drinking straw tube to make sure it seals perfectly.

how-to | # twirl stems around a paper frame

Create a guiding shape for the wreath by cutting out a circle from thick cardboard.

Remove all foliage from the weaving stems. Wrap the stems around the cardboard by bending them over the edge of the cardboard circle. Be careful not to break the fragile stem. Secure the stem by wrapping the next stem over the stem end.

Wrap the stem around the cardboard, following its shape. Add another stem by hooking it under the previous stem and continue to wrap.

Set the wreath out in the sun to dry completely.

Remove the cardboard by soaking the wreath in warm water to make it soggy and easy to rip away. Carefully lift the wreath from the water and set aside to dry out.

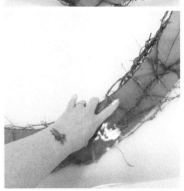

how-to | # bamboo and hollow stems

All natural and ready to use.

You can plug one end with wax or a cork stopper if the bamboo is open at both ends.

how-to | # balloons

Roll up the balloon a bit more and fill with water.

Insert the flower stem.

how-to | # bags

Small bags that seal are really convenient to use as a water source.

Slip the stem into the bag, add water, and seal it closed as tightly as possible with the stem in the bag . You can seal the bag with a constrictor knot, if necessary.

This provides ample water, and the bag adjusts to the available space.

how-to | # decorative, vintage, laboratory or empty perfume bottles

Rinse the bottles out, and you are ready to design.

how-to | # clear flexible pipes

Create intricate tangles with pipes. Make sure the two ends of each pipe are at the same height so that the water doesn't spill out.

how-to | # hollow and water tight treasures you find

Almost any hollowed-out, watertight container (found treasure) can be used as a water source. Always be on the lookout for an object that you can claim for this purpose and try it in a design if it speaks to you. And if it is not naturally watertight as it is found, see the following.

how-to | # dip in wax

You can create a watertight barrier on almost any surface or object by dipping it in melted candle wax, or pouring wax into the object and pouring it out again.

fruits, pods, gourds and vegetables

🌿 Fruits and vegetables emit ethylene gas, which causes the flowers in the design that are close to them to deteriorate faster.

🌿 This can be minimized, to some extent, by dipping the fruits in wax, which creates a thin barrier.

🌿 But mostly you can design without the wax layer, just be aware that it will not last as long as your other designs.

how-to | design in a pepper

Cut a cavity into the fruit with a sharp knife.

Line it with plastic, and then add a water source such as water tubes, a sandwich plastic bag filled with water, or floral foam.

Tuck in the plastic lining's edges so that the lining is not visible.

Add floral details, and make sure all the stem-ends are in water.

mastery
learning those techniques and developing your skills

"what looks like effortless craftsmanship
is actually a truly masterful craftsman
who has the ability to skillfully camouflage
exactly how much effort is put into crafting their art."

A creative designer needs a strong core of tried-and-tested techniques that can be relied upon when crafting.

The how-tos in this chapter are techniques that are fundamental to my own work and are in line with my approach to floral art. Some were taught to me when I was studying, some I taught myself as a little girl playing with flowers, some are treasured traditional craft techniques, and some I make up as I go along.

Practice these (and, of course, those techniques that you identify as central and foundational to your own art) like a musician practices scales. Musicians don't just play beautiful music. They practice the scales. They get those basics right. And then move on to a more advanced level. They master that level. And then move on to the next level. And once in a while they practice those scales again, investing the time to truly hone the basics. This is mastery. This is how you give your creative efforts the best chance of success.

Build your skill set to include those tried-and-tested traditional techniques even if your ambition is to be a contemporary designer. Practice wiring flowers even if you mostly use glue in designs. You need to know how. It gives you options and credibility.

Once you master a technique, you can expand, combine, and personalize it to create your own masterful art.

Of course, you do not need to know absolutely everything before you start creating. There is always more to learn. That really is part of the fun! Keep searching for stuff you don't know how to do, yet. The more you practice how to, the more reliable how-tos you will have in your tool bag of creative resources to draw upon when inspiration hits.

petaling and leafwork

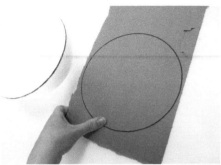

how-to | # edge-side-in, throat-side-out composite rose

Cut a circle out of sturdy cardboard.

For my design, I glued the petals with the edge of the petal facing in.

Start at the outer edge of the cardboard and glue petals all the way around.

Move inward and continue to glue petals to the cardboard.

For the innermost bit, firmly grasp a rose and pull the petals. Glue the entire rose, throat-side-out, to the cardboard.

how-to

composite rose foliage bowl

Roll the leaves in a similar way as you would a petallette.

Glue the cone-shaped leaves to the half-ball Styrofoam shape.

Start at the edge and glue leaves all the way around.

Move in and glue leaves in circles all the way in to the bottom of the bowl.

Set aside to dry and fill in any gaps created by the leaves shriveling.

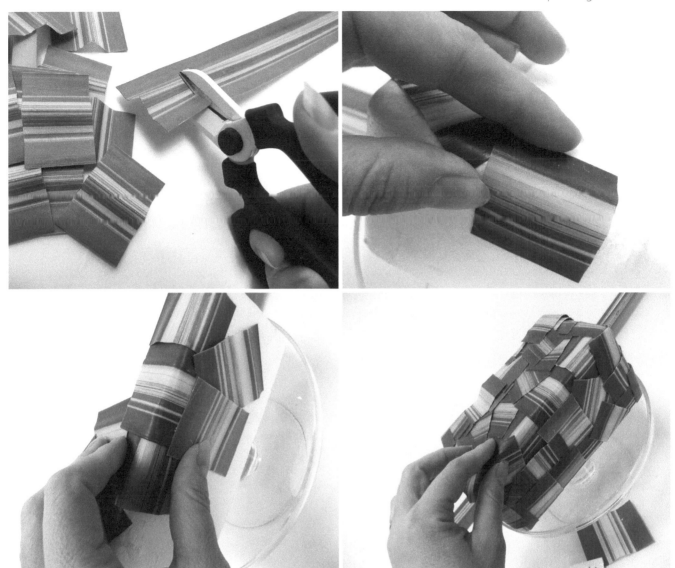

how-to | leaf snippet cube

Cut the leaf into snippets.

Glue the leaf snippets to a Styrofoam cube.

Smooth down each snippet to create a neat, flat coverage.

Create a random pattern by overlapping the snippets to ensure the cube will still be neatly covered after the leaf snippets shrink as they dry. No Styrofoam should show.

pierced, threaded, stacked, and skewered

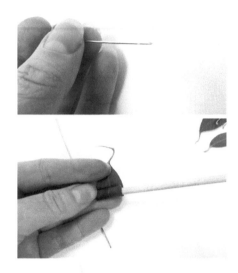

how-to | ## pierce foliage

Cut a thin wire at a sharp angle to make it easy to cleanly pierce through the leaves.

Roll a leaf around a dowel stick so that all the leaves are exactly the same size.

Pierce the leaf with the wire.

how-to | ## pierce fruits and vegetables with wire or skewers

Cones, vegetables, pods, and fruits can be skewered or wired to be added into the design.

Make sure any juices or sap is kept to a minimum by sealing the wound with floral glue or covering the fruit with a thin layer of wax.

how-to | # knot a twig to the end of the line

Tie a small twig at the end of fishing line, and thread the other end through the eye of a needle.

The short twig keeps the garlands from slipping out of the thread.

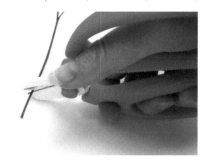

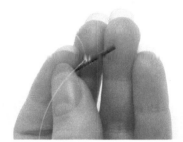

how-to | # make your own wire hairpin needle for threading flowers

Bend a tiny hairpin loop in the top end of the wire.

Bend the loop flat with pliers.

Cut the other end at a sharp angle.

Thread fishing line through the loop.

Use the hairpin wire needle to thread stems, leaves, berries, and flowers.

Carefully guide the flowers over the top, taking care not to rip them.

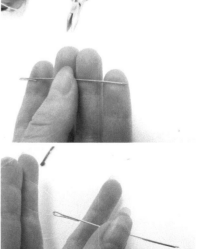

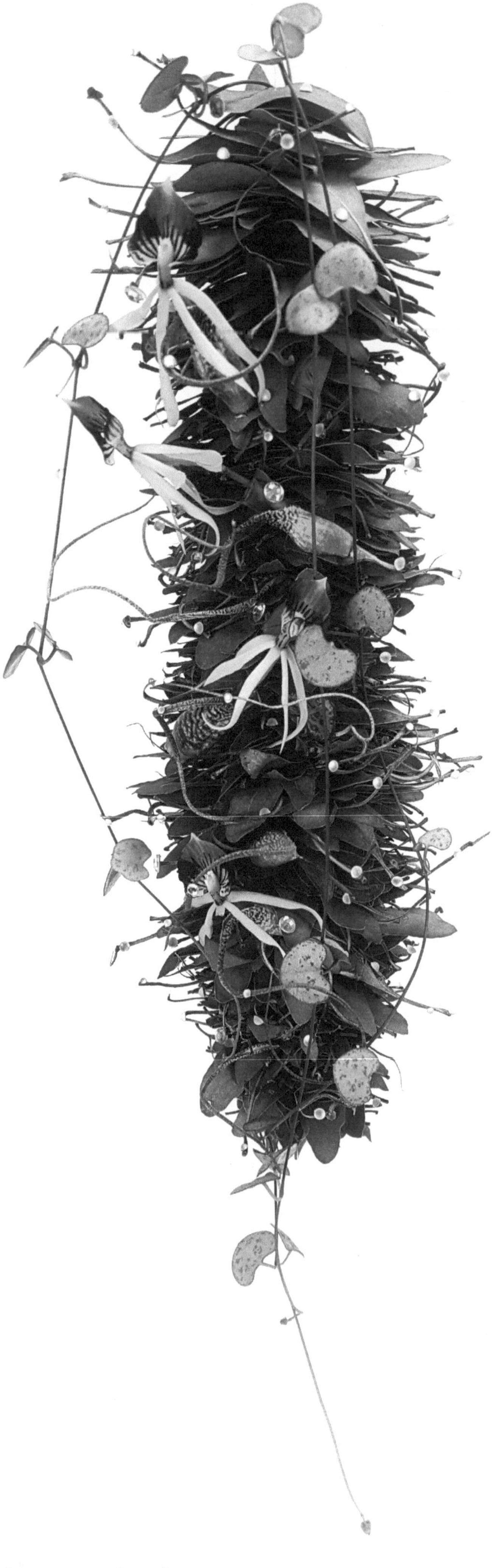

how-to

stack a eucalyptus leaf garland

Tie a small twig to one end of the line.

Thread the line through the eye of a needle.

Pierce the leaves to fill the length of the line.

Place the fresh flowers in water tubes (I concealed the tubes with air plants).

Add the dewdrop crystals and a few rosary vines.

how-to | ## stitch a leaf garland

Tie a small twig at the end of fishing line and thread the other end through the eye of a needle.

Stitch the eucalyptus leaves into a long garland.

The short twig keeps the garland from slipping out of the thread.

how-to | ## place the flowers and leaf garland in a shallow container with a kenzan

Place a Kenzan in the container.

Coil the garland into a spiral and set it in the container.

Place a few more leaves around the edge of the spiral to conceal the thread.

Pour water into the container and place the flowers and grass.

how-to | wire leaf garland

Cut one end of a wire into a sharp angle to cleanly pierce the leaves.

Curl the other end with pliers to keep the leaves from slipping off.

Pierce the leaves and curl the wire in, to secure.

Curve the two ends of the wire into a half moon.

Set the leaf garland into a container. Glue a leaf over the wire at both ends to conceal.

Fill the container with water and add the fresh flowers.

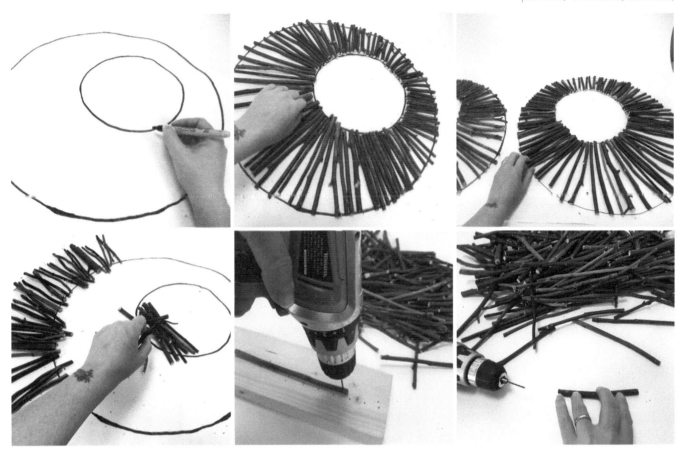

how-to | thread a twig handbag

Draw the outline of the handbag.

Draw a large circle with a smaller circle inside it.

Measure and cut the twigs to fit inside the circle, radiating out.

You need two times the twigs to fit side by side in the circle. Then cut and place more twigs to fit side by side, radiating out and around just over half the circle to craft the sides and bottom of the handbag.

Drill a hole on both sides of every twig.

Measure out the holes so that they are approximately the same distance from the end on each twig.

Make a hook on one end of a wire to catch and secure the twigs.

Wire the inside holes first. Start in the midpoint of the smallest twigs and work your way around. Press the first small twig all the way through the length of the wire to lay securely next to the hook you made.

Continue all the way around.

When all the inside circle twigs are wired, loop the wire around the hook. Pull tight and

secure with another hook to close the circle.

Space out all the twigs and make sure the twigs lie flat. Bend the wire if required.

Start wiring the second circle of twigs. Again, wire only the inside circle holes. Secure the wire as was done with the first circle.

To wire the outer circles: place the two circles on top of each other. Cut two lengths of wire. Again, make a hook catch on each wire. Start in the middle of the smallest twigs and thread the wire through a few twigs. Do the same with the top twigs. Continue to work your way down and around the twigs.

When you reach about halfway down on the side, start to add some of the loose twigs that you kept aside to be the bottom twigs.

Wire a bottom twig between the circle twigs.

Now wire a top circle twig, one of the loose twigs, and then a bottom circle twig.

Keep adding twigs, wiring all the way around to the level point on the other side.

Continue to wire the outer circle twigs at the smaller, top side of the handbag. Pull the wire tight. Secure the wire by looping it at the first twig and wire hook. Bend the wires to shape the handbag and decorate with flowers.

lei making

My floral crown design is inspired by the first lei I learned how to make in Hawaii: by threading a single strand of dendrobium orchids.

how-to | ## lei making needle

A professional lei-making needle is about 15 to 30 cm long (mine is 15 cm, about 6in) and is pointed on one side and hooked on the other end to make it easier to thread and unhook the thread when done.

If you do not have a lei-making needle, look for the longest embroidery needle you can find or bend one from wire.

how-to | ## lei making thread

Fishing line, waxed dental floss, thin ribbon, or crochet thread will all work well. Basically any line that is smooth and will not damage the flowers as you thread it through.

Cut the thread as long as you want the lei to be, plus some extra length for knots. Be generous. You can always cut it shorter.

how-to | ## thread a palm spiral

Roll the palm leaf around the needle into a spiral and then thread it into the lei.

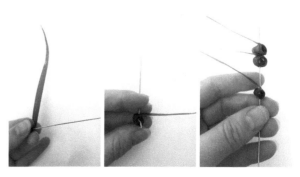

how-to | # thread dendrobium orchids

Dendrobium orchids look like they were created to be strung up, especially the bigger flowers.

Thread the needle and knot a small stem at one end to secure the flowers.

Cut the orchids from the stem. Cut away the entire stem and place the flower on a damp cloth. Mist with water. You will need about 50 orchids for a 50-cm-long (20in) lei, or less if you add other design details in the garland.

I like to place the floral details as I plan to thread them so that I know beforehand that there are enough of everything. Try to handle each orchid as little as possible. Be gentle. The less you fuss with the orchids, the less chance the flowers will break and bruise.

Push the needle into the throat of the orchid and out through the stub on the back. You can also reverse this halfway through to have a lei with both sides of flowers pointing up. Or you can thread the flowers through the sides as a variation.

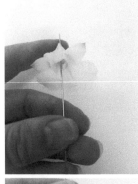

Position the flower as you pull it down the thread and leave it where it settles. It gracefully nestles in with the others.

I placed the garland facing away from me, lying flat on the damp washcloth so that it is protected. Don't move the flower garland. Rather, move each flower to the garland.

Slip or cut the thread from the needle and knot to the other end to secure. You can either keep or remove the stem you used as a knot on the other end to keep the flowers from slipping through the thread.

I conceal the knot by letting it slide into the throat of the orchid, but you can also add a ribbon to conceal it.

how-to | store the lei

Try to touch the flowers as little as possible to prevent bruising.

Make the lei close to the time you will wear it.

Place on a damp towel while working and mist the flowers often.

Once done, mist the flowers and place between slightly damp paper towels, in a cool place until you are ready to wear your lei.

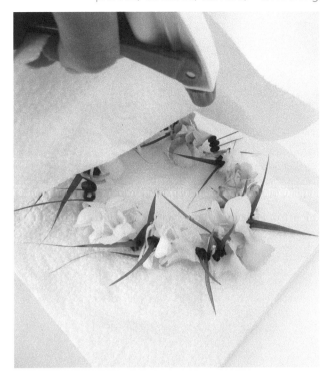

how-to | wear a lei

"Anytime," is the correct answer to: "when do you wear a lei in Hawaii?" Leis are worn at celebrations and are also worn by locals on a day as special as today.

A lei is often given as a gift. It is considered rude to not accept a lei, or to take one off in front of someone who offered it to you.

Drape the lei over your shoulders so that it hangs down both in the back and in front. Craft a shorter lei (like this one) to wear as a floral crown.

how-to | roll and secure a leaf with its own stem

Make a small guide hole in an autumn leaf with a bamboo skewer.

Roll the leaf stem up and slip it through the hole.

Slip the stem all the way through the hole and roll the leaf in.

Wrap the stem around the leaf to secure.

Make a new guide hole at the top end of the leaf with the bamboo skewer.

Slip the stem through the hole and carefully pull it tight to secure the roll.

how-to | ## glue leaves to a foam wreath frame

I covered the foam wreath frame with paper to create a barrier for the glue and to give the design a foundation colour that complements the design.

Soak yellow tissue paper in thinned wood glue.

Smooth the tissue paper over the frame.

Set the frame aside to dry completely.

Glue the leaves to the frame.

Wiggle a few rolled leaves between the glued ones to create a completely random pattern.

Let the stems point in all directions.

Set the wreath aside so that the leaves can dry. The leaves will shrink, leaving gaps for water tubes for the flowers, and more fresh leaves.

Tuck a few small water tubes deep into the leaves to keep the flowers hydrated and add a few more leaves to create depth.

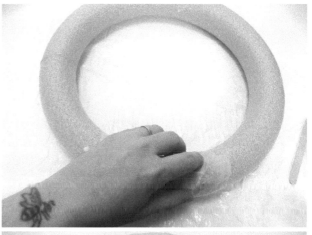

weaving

how-to

weave grass

To weave is to interlace bands, strands, or strips of material at right angles to build up a patterned mat, surface, or sculptural form.

I mainly use a balanced, plain weave pattern that looks like a checkerboard. This is often described as a one-up-one-down weave or an over-and-under pattern. There are many other weaving patterns, but I find this to be the most versatile because it is quick to do and doesn't compete for attention with my flowers.

Place a few blades of grass in a parallel horizontal position.

Weave a vertical pattern, with a new blade of grass, under and over the horizontal pieces.

Weave the second row, with a new blade of grass, over and under the horizontal pieces. Keep the weaving tight up against the previous row for a strong weave.

Handle with care—the weave will loosen up if it is not finished off.

To finish the weave:

Look carefully at the mat to catch the strip next to the one you are bending and weave it under the next possible blade. Flip the mat over and do the same on the other side until all the loose blades of grass are woven in.

how-to | choose and prepare phormium for weaving

Most decorative grasses can be woven without any preparation. But flax needs a bit of special attention.

Do not cut in rain or at night. The foliage will be hard to work with because of the added moisture.

Let the leaves dehydrate for a while so that they are soft and pliable.

Hold the dull underside of the leaves against the back of your knife and pull through. Turn the leaf over and do the other side. This removes added moisture, and the leaf will dry to a better colour.

how-to | guide blades of grass

I use a cuticle pusher to guide the blades of grass when I weave.

It is also an excellent tool to reposition the grass.

how-to | interweave

Interweaving follows the same basic rules as weaving, but you just add grass in all directions, some over a few blades and some under.

how-to | weave a basket

Rip a palm or flax leaf into sections to remove the thicker vein from the middle section of the leaf.

Weave the base of the basket to the required size and fold all the leaves sharply up.

Gather the leaves and either set them down loosely or tie them with an elastic band.

Continue the weaving pattern along the sides of the basket by following what was done for the base, again sharply folding the leaf at the corners.

Finish off the basket by overlapping the end pieces, weaving each piece back into the basket to secure.

how-to | weave a ribbon into the basket

For my design, I wove a ribbon into the basket. Follow the weaving pattern and simply add the ribbon. Before securing the ribbon in a knot or bow, weave another leaf above it to give the basket its shape.

how-to | weave an edge

The simplest way to create an edge, or finish off a weave, is to fold the strands and weave them back into the basket.

Continue the weaving pattern and catch the top strand either over to the front or over to the back. Weave the rest of the leaves and cut short to tidy it up.

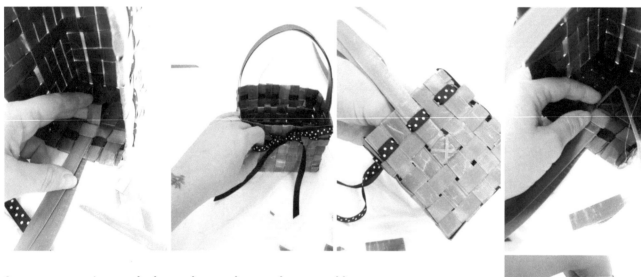

how-to | add a basket handle

Catch a strand in the basket with another leaf, fold it over, and weave it through the basket. Cross-tie the handle with a thin strand of leaf or grass to secure.

how-to | weave a box

The easiest way to weave a box is to use a form—something to weave around. I used two cube vases, one slightly larger than the other.

Place an elastic band around the vases to secure them for a stable form.

For the box, I am using the smaller vase. Weave the base so that the vase fits on top of it.

Fold the leaves up and keep them in place with the elastic bands.

Weave the sides, following the basic weaving pattern that you used on the base.

When the box is as big as you want it, fold the strands to score a straight line at the edge.

Continue the weaving pattern and catch the top strand either over to the front or over to the back. Weave the rest of the leaf and cut short to tidy it up.

how-to | weave a lid

Use the larger vase to size the lid.

Do not weave all the way down. Weave about three or four strands.

Fold the strands over and weave it back on itself to secure.

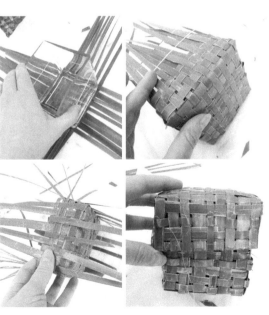

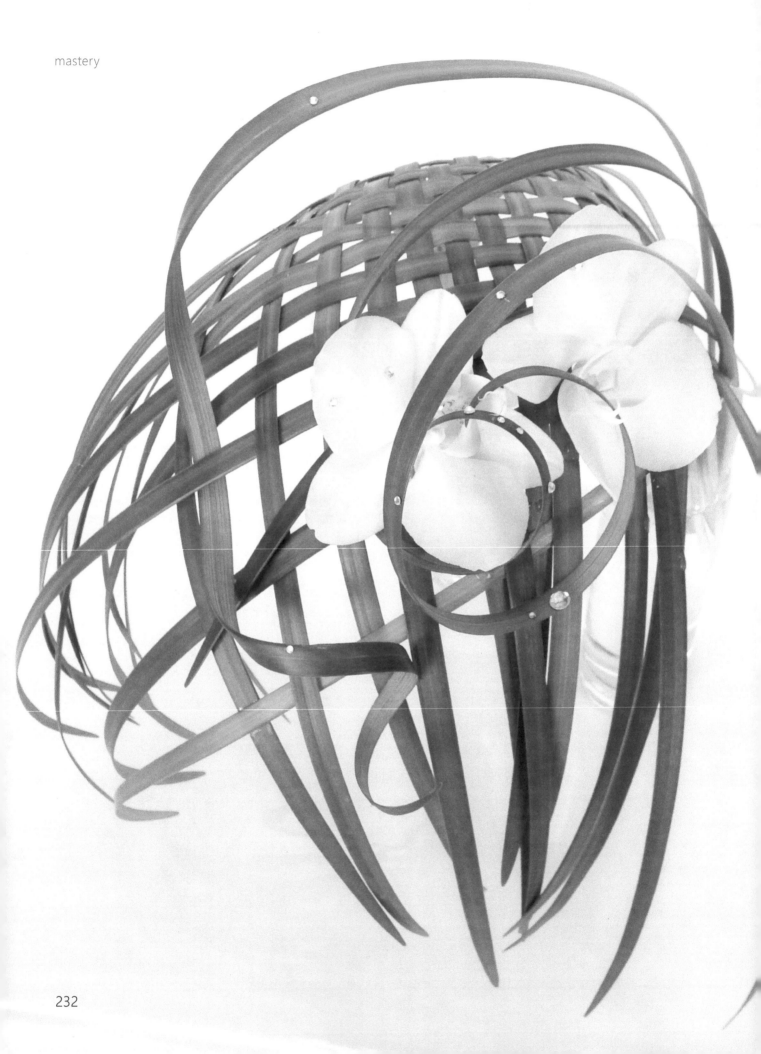

how-to | weave a grass parachute

Place a few blades of grass in a horizontal position on a flat working surface.

Start to weave blades of grass.

I used a simple over-and-under pattern.

Adjust the weave to secure with the blunt side of a cuticle pusher.

Extend the stems to the side at a wide angle.

Cut the stems to the same length.

Gather the stem ends in your hand.

Carefully lift the woven grass as a unit.

Set the stems in two vases filled with water.

Adjust the weave with the blunt side of a cuticle pusher.

Add the fresh flowers, curled grass, and dewdrop beads.

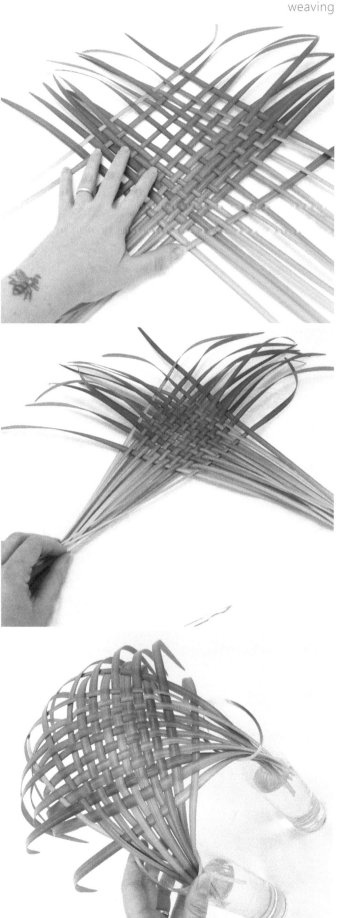

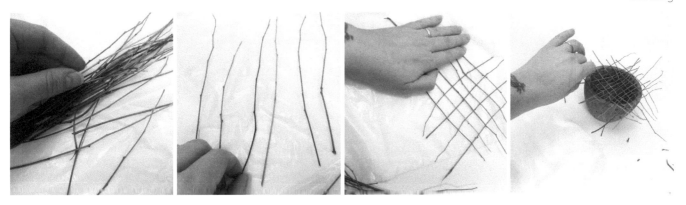

how-to | # weave a twig grid

Remove the foliage from a few weaving stems and set the stems flat on a working surface.

Weave the stems in an over-and-under pattern.

Place the stems over a container and fill the container with water. Then set the flowers to rest on the grid with the stems in water.

binding

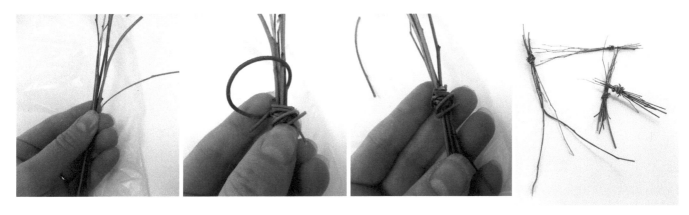

how-to | # bind twig bundles

Gather a few twigs.

Wrap a pliable stem around the twigs and knot it on itself.

Pull the knot tight and cut away the rest of the stem.

wrapping

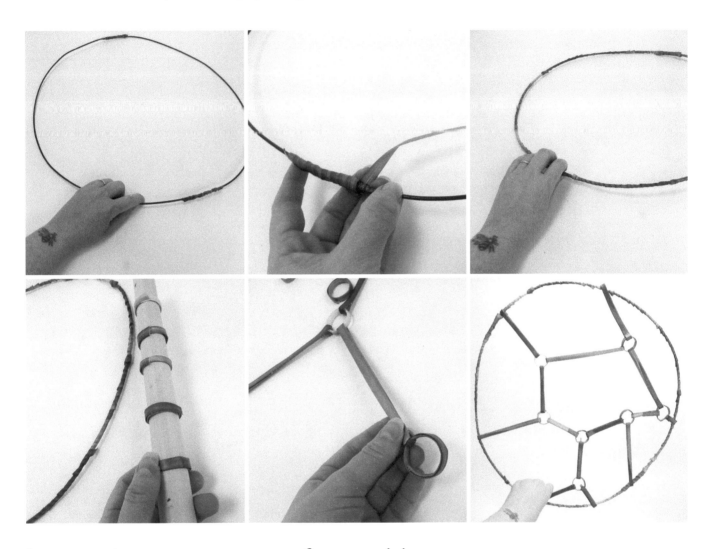

how-to | # wrap a grass-framed harness armature

Bend and secure a wire ring.

Wrap the ring with blades of grass.

Wrap and glue a few sections of grass around a dowel stick to create rings.

Fold a blade of grass over a ring and secure with glue.

Connect the grass rings to the wire ring with blades of grass to create a random pattern.

Hang the glass seahorses, or water tubes, and add the fresh flowers.

winding

how-to | wind a wire and grass ring basket

Twist eight decorative wires together to create 16 radiating spikes.

For this really delicate basket, I ripped foliage into fine strands.

Press the ends of a few strands of ripped leaf into a gap in the wire.

Fold the ripped foliage up to start the winding pattern.

Fold the strands of grass behind the wire and wind the strands of grass once around the wire.

Fold the strands of grass behind the next wire and wind.

This is the basic pattern. Continue winding the wire spiraling around and around from the inside out.

Do not change direction. Just continue winding around and around the decorative wire.

When you reach the end of a strand, simply add a few more strands and continue to wind. The longer strands will bind the ends of the previous strands.

Fold the wires up and continue to wind strands of grass to create the sides.

Simply wind the strands spiraling up to as high as you want the basket to be.

When the basket is high enough, wind the wire around the strands of grass.

Fold the strands of grass and wire to the side, and wind the next wire around the strands.

Work your way around the basket, securing the strands and the wire.

Cut any leftover strands away.

Neatly finish the design by winding a strand of grass to cover the wire around the rim.

Knot the strand of grass on itself and cut away any loose pieces.

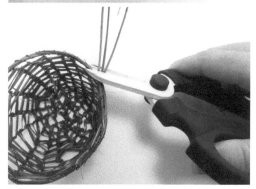

how-to | wrap, plait, and weave a willow parasol

Cut five lengths of sturdy wire to curve for the ribs of the parasol shape.

To weave the willow through the wires, you need an uneven number of wires, so after securing the middle with bind wire, bend one of the legs in for a handle.

Weave in thin willow stems through the wires to create a dense spiral around the binding point.

Plait three willow stems around the woven spiral to look like flower petals.

Secure the braided stems with thin willow. This is a looser weaving pattern. Wrap the stem around the wire once and extend it to the next wire. I also covered the exposed wire inside the braided petals by wrapping the wire with willow stems.

Bend the wire ends in with heavy-duty pliers and finish the looser weave right up to the bend.

Weave more stems all the way to the bottom and a few random stems curving over the parasol to create a wild and natural effect.

Wrap the handle with willow and add support stems where needed.

how-to | stretcher support for the willow parasol

Split a sturdy stem.

Slip the stem over the wire rib of the parasol.

Weave a willow stem around the support stems to secure them in place.

Turn the parasol over and tie the support stems so that you secure the design where it is split over the rib.

braiding

Braid and *plait* are synonyms, and where you are from will most likely dictate whether you use the word *plait* (British) or *braid* (American or Celtic). Some people also refer to cornrows as braids or refer to pinned-up plaits as braids. A French braid is a braiding technique.

A braid in floral design is a pattern created by interlacing strands of flexible material such as pliable twigs, grass, or fibers.

Plaiting with plant material is harder to do than plaiting with ribbon and string, because the strands break easily, are naturally less pliable in places, and they vary in width. Its best to just let nature curve and bend as you go along.

To make it easier for yourself, simply tape the foliage to a working surface so that it doesn't slip around.

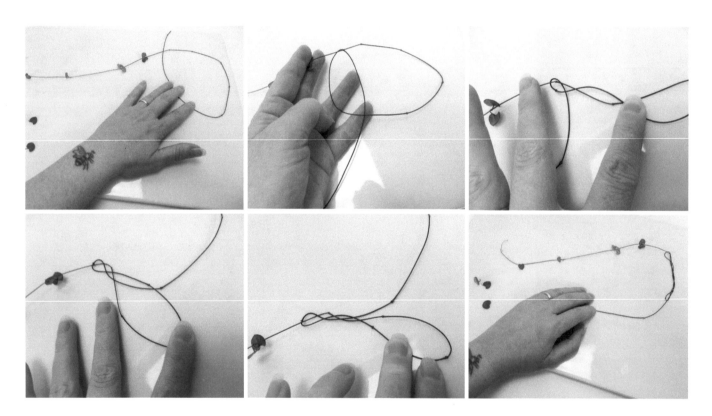

how-to | # single strand braid

Loop the strand. This loop will determine how long the braid is.

Make a loose knot.

Twist the loop to create the next hole and push the strand through.

Twist again and push the strand through until you reach the end of the loop.

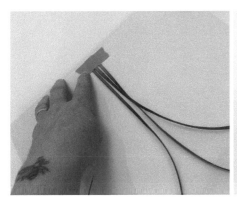  

how-to | three strand braid

Tape the strands to a working surface.

Cross outside right over the middle and under outside left, and then cross outside left over the middle and under outside right.

That is the basic pattern. Repeat to finish the braid.

 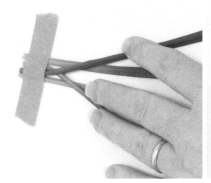 

how-to | four strand braid

Tape the strands to a flat working surface. The secret with this braid is to only move two strands at a time.

Start braiding with the middle strands, crossing the strand middle left over middle right.

Middle left goes over outside left and middle right under outside right.

Cross middle left over middle right and then middle left over outside left and middle right under outside right.

That is the basic pattern. Repeat to finish the braid.

how-to | braid a palm thorn garland

Split the leaf with a corsage pin along the main vein in the middle of the leaf. Then split both sides in two.

Tape the leaf to your working surface with masking tape.

Start the braiding pattern by folding the outer leaf in and around the strong vein, then fold the opposite leaf in and around the vein.

Continue the braiding pattern. Fold the outermost leaf in and around on one side and then the other.

Either knot the end pieces, or weave them in on themselves.

Cut the dangling leaf bits short.

Cut into the leaf to give it dramatic thorns.

how-to | rip flax

After harvesting the flax leaves, set them aside to dehydrate slightly. If you condition them in water, they will be very moist when ripped. I prefer not to let them dehydrate in full sun because that causes the leaves to roll up, making it harder to pull through the Kenzan teeth.

Wipe the leaf clean and cut the hard stem away. Cut into thin strips.

Place the Kenzan (pin cushion) on the edge of your working surface. With the palm of your hand, press the lower end of the leaf to catch in the teeth.

Drag the leaf down and through the nails.

The ripped sections will first dry to a beautiful grass green, then a grey green, and later a stone green.

design note | braid the ripped flax to coil for the sandals

coiling

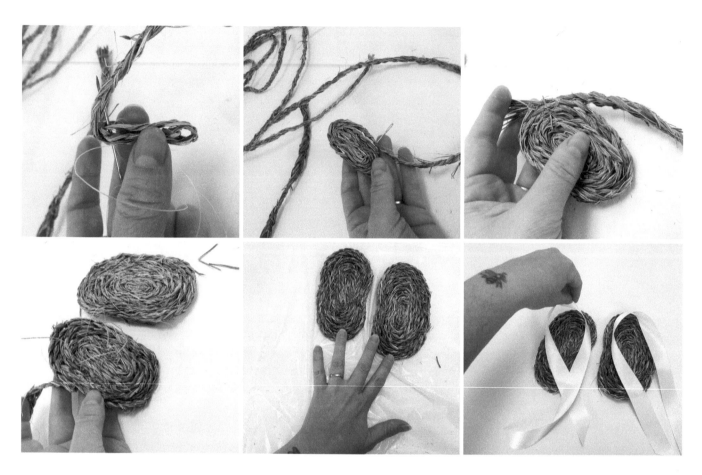

how-to | # coil sandals with braided ripped flax

Start to coil the braided flax strand. I stitched it as I went along with fishing line threaded through an embroidery needle.

Build up the sole.

Fold the braid over and create a slightly wider toe section of the sandal.

Finish by coiling the braid around the sandal. Stitch through the entire sandal and pull tight to shape it. Knot the line to secure.

Set it aside to dry.

Measure out ribbon for each sandal.

Cut two sections of ribbon for each sandal.

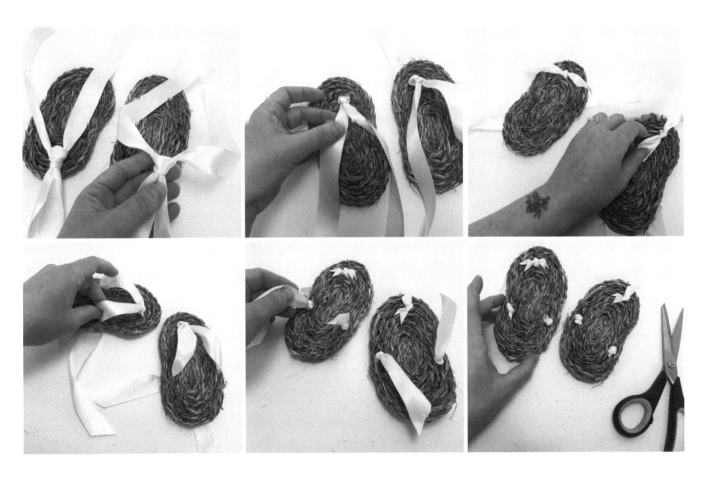

Loop one ribbon around the other at the midpoint, in a lark's head knot.

Pull tight to knot.

Slip the ribbon through the sandal sole and catch it over the coil.

Turn the sandal over and knot tightly to secure the ribbon.

Do the same with the other sandal.

Fold the ribbon over to the front of the sandal, over the bridge of the foot.

Flip the sandal over and knot tighly around the loop on the side.

Cut the ribbon ends short and wiggle the knots to sit snugly in the sole.

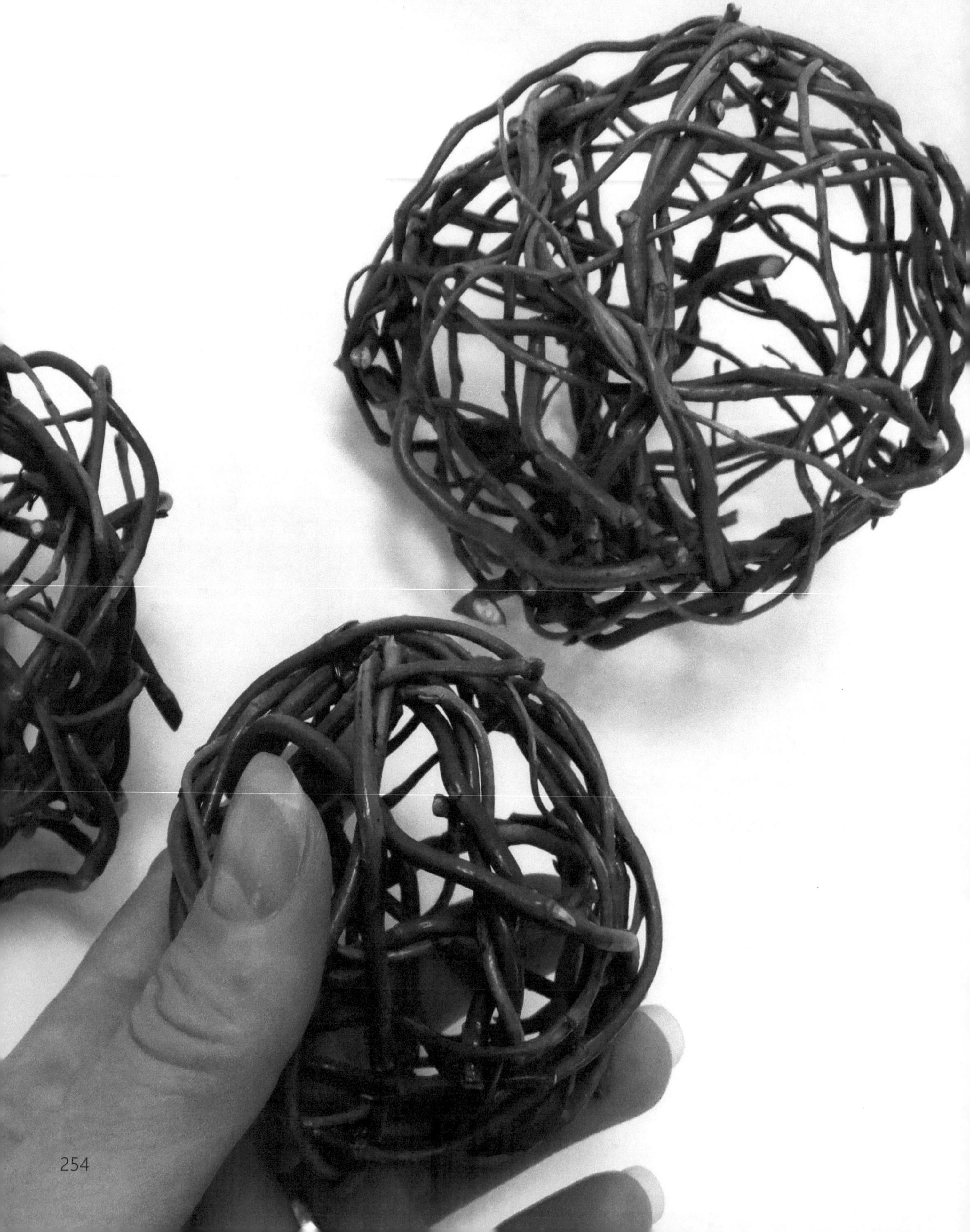

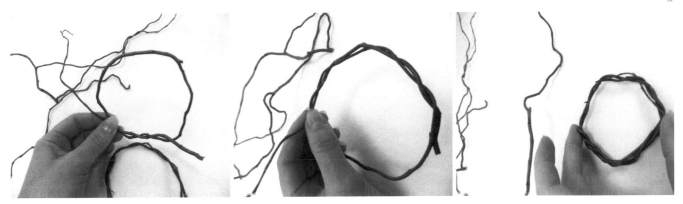

how-to | weave a wreath

It is easy to scale up, or down, the size of your wreath.

Bend a pliable stem into a circle as big as you want the wreath to be and weave the rest of the stem in and out so that it twirls around the circle.

Hook another stem into a gap in between the twirled twig and continue to weave the stem around the circle to build up the wreath to the required thickness.

how-to | interweave willow spheres

To build up a ball or sphere, use soft and flexible willow to weave about five small wreaths.

Slip one wreath over a second to start building up the ball shape and secure with wire.

To break up the wreath lines, I weave in long stems of thin, pliable willow. Weave the willow in and out, randomly twining it around and around the ball.

effortless style

*"effortless designing is not so much easy as it is
unforced, natural, and graceful.
the closer you are to designing as you, the more effortless the result."*

Have you ever seen someone play a musical instrument so well that it looked unbelievably easy? Or watched a top athlete perform at his peak and find yourself foolishly thinking, *How hard can that be?*

Have you had the opportunity to attend a demonstration of a really masterful designer who made creating truly brilliant designs look effortless?

What is it that makes these masterly efforts look so easy?

For work to be effortless, you need three things: know-how, know-who, and a worthy what. You need a deep understanding of how, so that you can focus your creative energy on adding your own unique, you specific, unmistakable who to a what that you consider worthy enough of your effort to make it really special, every time.

Up to now this book has looked at acquiring the necessary skills and a thorough knowledge of the techniques (and stocking up on a few tools) needed to master our floral craft. But truly remarkable work is not simply a combination of a few flawlessly executed techniques. Remarkable comes from the artist adding something so uniquely "them" that the work takes a technique that we have seen so many times before and makes it sparkle. That is effortless style.

Quite simply, knowing how to design frees you up to create your design. Obvious? Maybe. But what I am trying to say is that even though our training is important, it is not where creative mastery ends. Only you can teach yourself how to create like only you can. This lesson can't be taught to you by anyone else. It is not a technique. It is the way you use your tools, skills, and techniques.

I am sure by now you are starting to suspect that making hard work look effortless is going to require quite a lot of effort.

The good news is that you have always been doing it. You already have an effortless style of designing. There will be hints to this, even as a beginner designer chooses to do her very first design. In this chapter I look at how to recognize it, protect it, then exaggerate it, and ultimately make the you-ness deliberate and obvious.

How do we recognize what effortless designing feels like?

It is the feeling that happens in those moments when we are crafting our work and forget all about technique and our talent takes over. You have found the floral design equivalent of when the scissors just start to glide through wrapping paper. You are in your creative zone. Let me explain:

- Let's say you've got this. You know how to make what you are currently making. You have done it so many times before that it is ... well ... quite honestly, boring. But you are making it, again. The end result might be a flawlessly executed technique, but there will be nothing remarkable about it. The idea has lost its sparkle. You become bored if you are constantly designing things that are too easy for you. This kind of craft is not effortless. In fact, it is quite taxing to create something that does not inspire you.

- Let's say you jump right over aiming for "gold" and go for "platinum." You have no idea how to do this and you attempt a technique that is quite a leap from where you are now. It starts out quite exciting but soon turns into a bundle of frustration. It is just too hard to figure out. And now you are discouraged and exhausted. Effortless? Bah!

- Effortless designing happens somewhere in the middle of these two extremes of the craft. It is a bit of "I got this" with a bit of "go for gold." You know how to do this. Well, not exactly this. Not yet. But you are confident because you have learned a technique that would be perfect for this. And besides, you are curious to see if you can pull it off. You are challenged just enough to be stimulated and energized. You are on the path to mastering your craft. You use the techniques you are comfortable with and improvise to add your bit to it. Before you know it, you have completely lost track of time and things just naturally flow, effortlessly. You are crafting a design just slightly better than you thought you could possibly do. You feel it in your gut, and you want to return to this feeling.

design note | want to know whether you just did a design slightly better than you thought possible?

Answer: Did you take a picture of it?

It is as simple as that. I do this. And I have seen it over and over when other designers do this at shows. If you just outdid yourself, you are going to want to take a picture.

Do you not even bother to bring a camera along anymore? Well, then ...

Developing a unique technical style becomes yet another tool for you to add to your tool bag of resources for when you craft your work.

It is not found outside of yourself. How-to training should never include style. Style is what you bring to the training.

Look at it this way: if your techniques and skills are your eyes, your style would be the magnifying glasses you use to see clearly. You can design with your learned skills and techniques alone, of course you can. But it is your unique style that adds that creative twist to the techniques and brings your work into focus. It is with your style that you push the limits of skills and techniques and expand on those limits, creating the elements that make your work remarkable.

Emulating someone else's style is exhausting and leads to a state of dis-ease (pun intended). Being true to your own style requires much less energy because you are at ease and your actions are natural. Your efforts appear effortless.

Don't fight these design instincts. If you have a quirky way of doing something, celebrate it. Don't force a way of executing a technique if it feels uncomfortable. Find your own way.

Please be protective over that unique spark that makes you, you. Nurture your aptitude so that it grows and blossoms into art.

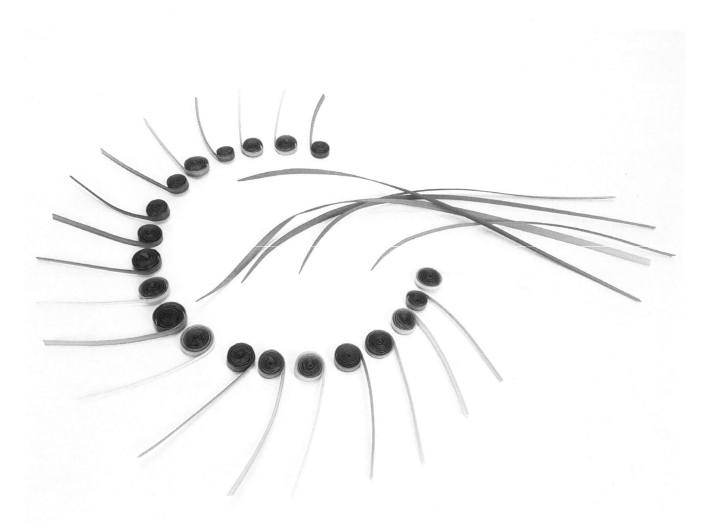

And if you have been crafting for a while and find that your creative spark is a little bashed and bruised?

Give yourself some space. Shut down the criticism and the have-tos and have a bit of fun. Just like plant material always behaves and reverts to its natural state, so do you. It takes extreme, constant pruning and wiring to convince a bonsai tree to remain small. You grow and change all the time (of course you do!) into new versions of yourself. I would have written a considerably different book just a few years ago. It would have still been mine, but different. I have figured out some stuff since then. And I am figuring out stuff now. But what I am trying to say is that you have a certain style about you that is so uniquely you—if you give yourself enough room and freedom to create in, you will revert to your natural style of design even if you can't recognize it now by looking at the shape it's in.

If understanding how plant material responds to trauma is the heart of all of our techniques, then mastering the art of deliberately adding our personality to our work is the heart of being a craftsman. Adding your own personality to your work requires introspection. But it is the only true way to add heart to your work.

People often say creating distinctive art comes with experience, by which I think they mean it comes from working with respect, and with great sensitivity, awareness, and intention. Working regardless and relentless, and having grit to stay at it and show up whether you feel like it or not. But yes, experience is a good (not so intimidating) word. Because with experience you become more skilled, which brings more comfort. In those moments when you are comfortable doing your work, you add yourself. It is impossible not to. As we discover those things that make up our style, we exaggerate them into our distinctive art.

Here is a short list of ideas to explore that may have an influence on you, and your effortless style.

Finding your you-ness:

- Look at how the floral culture you are exposed to and live in affects your design decisions. Also look at the places you have visited or where your loved ones come from. Places you would like to visit or have a strange and unexplained connection to. Places and cultures leave an impression on our talent.

- What are you interested in? Look at both professional and hobby experiences. The skills you have learned are often transferable and give you a unique perspective. Where interests overlap is often where innovation happens.

- Availability of plant material. Are you working close to a garden, nursery, or farm? Often when we see an abundance of something specific in a designer's work, it could be a personal preference, or it could quite simply be because it is readily available in the artist's environment.

- Your abilities and natural skills.

- Your self-developed or adopted design philosophies.

- Your personal preferences.

Is there anything that jumps out at you? Take that and explore it. See how you can add your own creative style (such as ideas, heritage, personality, and taste) and your technical style (such as mannerisms, dexterity, physical abilities, stamina, grit, experience, and habits) to your work.

Ultimately, we all want to craft work that is so distinctive that it has our name written all over it.

Your best work is that which could only be crafted by you.

I have discovered that I am somewhat ambidextrous.

For example, when I am really, really into a design, my hands are on their own mission. My left hand could be screwing back the cap of my glue, while my right hand continues to manipulate and position the plant material. The more focused I am, the more naturally this happens. It has become part of my style. The moment that I am made aware of it I become so self-aware that it stops or becomes an effort. Our muscles have memory. With repetitive practice, our hands seem to do the task with little to no input from our brain. If I am now stopped and asked to explain how I just did that, it interrupts the rhythm I was working in and it might even be difficult for me to verbalize even though I know this technique so well and did it perfectly a moment ago.

Somewhere within repetition, techniques became part of me. Which really is the goal.

Even daunting tasks become effortless with practice. So learn, practice, and then internalize your techniques. Once you know those how-tos, even those things that you might consider limitations at the moment can develop into slight alterations in the execution of techniques that will, over time, develop into an effortlessly creative strength. Your quirky way of crafting.

Marius once told me:

Trust your talent.

Words I design by

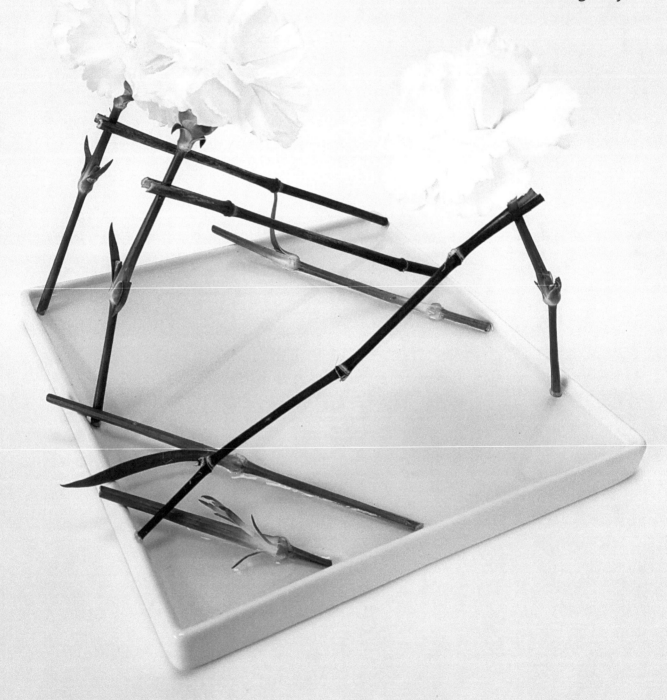

Effortless designing is a creative act of self-discovery and of course self-expression. It is also an act of self-creation.

You design with what you have. You discover your limitations, and you create your way around them.

As you learn, you change. We are not what we have always been. I don't believe we are people experiencing things. I believe the things we experience make us, well ... who we are. Which means you can take an active role in your creative development by searching out experiences, continually learning, adding techniques to practice, and pursuing interests that influence your unique style and creativity.

design note | ## cutting the stem before designing

If you design in a shallow container, such as this one, it is better to cut the stem flat (rather than at a sharp angle as you normally would) so that the entire cut area of the stem is under water.

PLEASE DO
NOT TOUCH

We know you appreciate the
effort that went into planning
and completing these designs.

Thank you!

CANADA

CHRISTINE DE BEER

NAFAS INTERNATIONAL BC

testing the rules

"creativity needs something to kick against..."

I am a huge fan of rules, in general. Rules set a standard of conduct. We know what to expect and what is expected of us.

I know now not to disregard all rules, however well or creative my intentions. But if you know only one thing of my personality, let it be this: I am made up of opposite things that are simultaneously true. I also believe that the rules never, ever tell us how to be exceptional at our craft. Better, yes. Exceptional, no. That is not what rules do. So, in this chapter I explore how intention tests rules.

When you study traditional crafts, you will notice that it is often compliance to a certain look or technique or style or unbending design rule that made them so enduring and gave them staying power to actually become valued enough to be considered something traditional. Think of a Hogarth curve design. A great amount of skill is involved in the creation of a perfect Hogarth curve, but it does not provide a huge scope for originality or creativity from the craftsman. It is always going to be a curve in an S (or inverted S) shape. You can already picture the design, probably in great detail. In fact, the more familiar you are with the design rules governing the specific craft, the greater your ability to visualize it in detail.

You also notice it when you look at contemporary designs. When you look at a leading-edge design and think, *That is amazing*, you cannot put your finger on exactly what makes the design work. But it just works. When you look at the next design, which looks as if there is something not quite right, the flaw usually stems from somehow forgetting (or not knowing) the rules.

Contemporary designers are valued because they move away from traditional rules to develop something, well ... contemporary.

As contemporary designs evolved and became more sophisticated as a style, the need for an even greater understanding of the traditional principles and elements of design grew. For example, proportions become harder to calculate if you are working with an armature rather than a vase, but it is still an important design consideration.

For even the most contemporary, unusual, and leading-edge designs to be really effective there should be some respect for- or consideration of- the rules. Simply ignoring the rules that are associated with traditional designing has become unworkable.

Competing in a competition is probably the quickest way to learn this. It is quite simple: misunderstanding or disregarding the rules in your competition schedule means all your hard work and preparations are wasted. If you are out of schedule, you have failed. Same goes for ignoring your design brief from a client. It is also true when it comes to the rules that govern your own design philosophy. Rules are rules, whether it is a rule you were taught or received or learned through personal experience by adapting and adjusting when you discovered something worthy of adapting and adjusting for.

But what are the rules?

It is unrealistic to believe that you create in a no-rule environment. Constraints will always apply in some form. See it as a way of leveling the playing field. Rules happen to all of us. It is by exploring the intention behind the rules that you will notice how many of our design rules guide us to create even better work.

Your designs, no matter how creative, should be immaculately crafted. That is one of those rules. And it is a good one. A few more examples are:

- A gift design should be easy to care for.
- A bridal design and body flowers should be comfortable, even luxurious (at best), and not dangerous or damaging (at least). It should be easy to carry, and lightweight.
- A centerpiece design should not block the view of the guests seated at the dinner table.
- A funeral tribute design should convey an emotion.
- A competition design should be in schedule.

All good rules.

design note | As a checklist, you can't go wrong with a basic competition marking sheet to see if your design follows the rules.

the guiding rules

competition marking sheet

Interpretation and understanding basic floral design:

- Does this design fulfill the requirements stipulated in the brief or schedule or what you set out to accomplish?
- Is it functional (if applicable)?
- Is it appropriate?

Making it your own/ distinction:

- Are you telling your floral story in your own creative voice?
- Originality.
- Choice of the materials used.

Principles of Design:
Major:

- Balance
- Dominance
- Proportion
- Rhythm
- Scale

Minor:

- Contrast
- Harmony
- Radiation
- Repetition
- Gradiation or Transition

Elements of Design:

- Line
- Pattern
- Form
- Space

- Texture
- Colour
- Fragrance
- Size

Craftsmanship:

- Condition of material.
- Presentation.
- Skills and techniques.
- Mechanics.
- Workmanship.

design note | as a rule of thumb

Contemporary design concepts grow out of:

- Inspiration to create something new

- Traditional design rules (such as principles and elements of design)

- A good and solid understanding of flower-arranging basics (such as our skills and techniques)

- The fact that floral design follows function (we sometimes craft stuff that gets used)

These rules are still around despite our best collective attempts to "creative " them into a thing of the past.

The rules are gifts from innovative designers who made the extra effort to find what was then groundbreaking ways to craft their art for us to use as stepping-stones along our own creative journey. It sounds almost easy to think that we can merely follow these rules and create art. This would not be our art. Our unique and creative art.

In my experience, creativity flourishes in an environment where it has something to kick against. Finding your own exception to the rules gives your creativity the kickstart it needs.

Some rules are easier to follow or disregard than others. If the rule is there for your benefit, it is foolish to disregard it. But all rules do not apply to all situations. There is no need to follow outdated design rules. Trends are most certainly not to be followed as rules, nor are styles or preferences. The trick is to figure stuff out for yourself, just like the groundbreaking craftsmen before you did.

Learning which rules are bendable and which rules break your art is part of mastering your craft. This is both painful and rewarding.

People often say, "You have to know the rules to break them." I understand what they mean, but I don't agree with the semantics. You can manipulate a rule. You can bend a rule. But you cannot break a rule. When you break a rule, it is usually you that gets broken ... or at least get fined, inconvenienced, disqualified, or penalized. The rule remains unaffected by your actions. The ways to ultimately break a rule are to: collectively disregard it, remove it, or replace it. Now that might be what is needed, but our intention here is not creating better or less rules. Our intention is innovation. Making art. We are deliberately setting out to create something new and groundbreaking in a craft form that has existed since creativity itself. That means it comes with a well-established set of rules. The only way for a contemporary craftsman to innovate is with intention.

Earlier I looked at testing the rules by looking at their intention. Let's look at our intentions regarding exceptions to the rules.

When testing whether there really is an exception to a rule, ask yourself what exactly you are doing with that rule:

- If you are manipulating the rules to serve yourself, you are probably well on your way to breaking your art (or getting disqualified or having a very unhappy client).

- If you are manipulating a rule to create something that would benefit or inspire the flower crafting community as a whole, you are ... well ... making groundbreaking art.

Work within the real constraints of crafting, and within the predetermined challenges of traditions, by studying, understanding, and regularly revisiting the rules. Find your exception to these rules that are in line with the way you are wired. Explore those boundaries to develop your own set of rules that seem effortless to you and groundbreaking to us. This will become your contribution to our craft and inspire the next generation of exception-finding craftsmen to again explore, expand, and challenge those rules.

design note | when faced with a design dilemma, ask yourself these four questions:

- How does nature make things?
- How does nature make the most of things?
- How does nature make things disappear?
- What would nature do?

crafting an illusion

"nature has already solved the problem you are struggling with in your design ... go look."

We have been expressing through art and crafting useful things from nature for a long, long time. We are crafting a story that can hold our berries or be displayed to bring comfort or worn to celebrate our milestones (more about this in the next chapters on Inspiration and Interpretation) with materials that grow and blossom and wilt and fade and dry. And we need them to grow and blossom and wilt and fade and dry. In order to plait tulip stems, the flowers must dehydrate and wilt ... just a bit. In order to get pods, flowers need to fade. For baskets to become sturdy, we need pliable stems to dry.

We study and test and develop our skills and prepare our flowers to create ecosystems that bring about the exact right conditions for our plant material so that we can craft our stories. This is the point where your knowledge of horticulture / botany and your skills in designing overlap. If you understand what happens to a plant in trauma and how to condition it, you understand what the plant is capable of. In this chapter we learn from nature, first how to design and then how to respectfully manipulate stems, twigs, branches, grasses, flowers, and finally leaves, petals, and foliage.

Crafting contemporary designs is all about crafting illusions. It is highly manipulated designs that appear natural. Fantastical, but natural. I like to imagine that my work can be discovered deep in an enchanted forest where anything is possible.

An armature can easily be incorporated into a traditional design by following the traditional designing guidelines. Imagine a woven sphere in a cascade design. But the reverse creates a disconnected effect. Adding a traditional design into a contemporary armature never really forms a natural-looking unit.

It is difficult to successfully transition between traditional and contemporary designing and can only be done by really observing nature from a new perspective.

Contemporary designing is a form of biomimicry, crafting with nature to create natural-looking designs using natural solutions to design problems as done by nature. A good foundation in traditional designing will train your eye and sharpen your design instincts. Both traditional and contemporary design take their inspiration from nature and then expand on that. As with traditional designing, successful contemporary work has its own design rules; they are merely less defined as they are part of a younger stage of the ongoing, organic, innovative process. We are still making it up.

Sometimes illusion is created by going the opposite way of what nature does or by exaggerating what nature does. Even then, we need to pay attention to nature's rules in order to find an exception that can be displayed in a believable way. A touch of the fantastic can highlight what is natural.

design note | principles and elements of design

Again, I find having a short checklist or marking sheet (such as those used for competition evaluations) is a great way to keep those more traditional principles and elements of design in mind while I am crafting.

That is your foundation. Creating the illusion is the next building block of contemporary design.

so, how does nature solve this problem?

Chances are, whatever you are trying to accomplish in your design, nature has already solved it. Observe animal and plant life. There you will find a natural solution for this, whatever your "this" is.

Tendrils curl to offer support. Seedpods shelter. Trees grow high because their trunks are thick at the bottom and the thinner, newer growth is at the top. Roots anchor plants to stop the plant from toppling over, creating a heavy base for a tall design. Dewdrops add sparkle. A meadow combines colours that inspire.

Fascinating advances in art, science, and technology use biomimicry. It is easy to find examples and to follow existing studies for inspiration.

These illusions are so convincing because you base them on what is actually real.

A good example of this would be creating a bark wreath. Now obviously there is no such thing as a doughnut tree, so you will not be able to harvest or grow this shape or look at one to mimic its design. But if you could ...

First, the bark would grow in the same direction, which is up, or in this case up and around. So, when you craft your wreath, glue the bark to face in the same direction, up and around.

really observe nature

What happens in a curve of a branch? Is there a way you can incorporate this in your design?

Then, when it comes to adding the flowers, ask yourself, *How would flowers grow in this imaginary doughnut tree?* Blossoms on the branches that grow out of the bark? Or maybe a vine spirals around the tree? It could even be an epiphyte nestled into a curve of the branch. Add your flowers to mimic this.

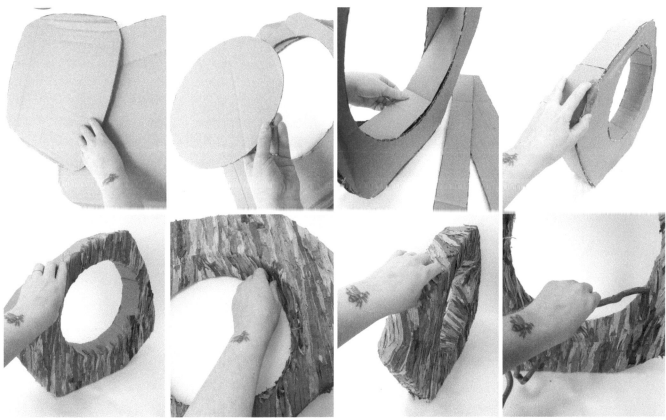

how-to | craft a doughnut tree wreath

Cut the basic shape out of sturdy cardboard.

Cut out the middle circles.

Connect the two halves with a strip of cardboard around the inside and the outside.

Rip bark into strips and glue them to the cardboard shape with hot glue.

Start with a flowing pattern, similar to a wood grain.

Follow the pattern to the inside and around the outside edge.

Glue in some twigs and add water tubes for the orchids, vines, and roots. Add crystals to finish off the design.

accessories

This really is up to you. Do whatever captures your imagination and design style. I love small, sparkling, dewdrop crystals. I have tried adding brightly coloured ones, but somehow always end up replacing them with the clear or more natural-looking crystals. This is just my taste. You might love the addition of decorative wire or baubles. Do whatever speaks to your own design style. Again, if this were to occur in nature, where would it be placed? Where would the sparkling dewdrops settle?

nature happens

You do not need to tell autumn to happen. It just happens. A bit of spontaneity in your design adds a natural element even if it is crafted. Don't be too perfect. Perfection defeats the purpose of living art. Stems curve naturally. Even when we manipulate stems, it really is only exaggerating what is already there. Drastically changing the natural curve of stems or branches requires extreme measures (such as wiring it to grow in that precise way, for example, bonsai trees or willow land art) as opposed to small manipulations that gently set them in a more pleasing direction. Again, we mimic what already exists. We cover wire by wrapping it with a pliable willow twig the way a tendril wraps itself around a support. Or we weave a stem the way a bird makes a nest.

Creating an illusion often requires manipulation in some shape or form. Be careful not to snap, harm, or bruise the plant material while manipulating. A healthy dose of respect for the plant is required when coaxing it into a different shape. It is important to know the characteristics and limitations of plant material. Some stems are easier to manipulate than others. Some flower stems can easily be woven into an armature, while others will offer resistance and just snap or return to their natural shape in time. How far you take the manipulation is up to you. One designer's plant mutilation is another designer's plant manipulation. Do you like dyed flowers? Only if it is not too obvious? Not at all? It is up to you.

when things grow up, things grow up

When adding tendrils or stems, make them mostly grow up. Any drooping stems create the impression of wilting, even if it is a dried design element. A good example of this is an oval wreath. Take care in your placement to exaggerate and enhance the shape so that is does not look like a bottom-heavy or wilting circle. Mimic healthy and flourishing nature. Flowers point to the light. If you are designing on location, this can be powerfully used to create a natural, "it just grew this way" look in a very manipulated design by carefully incorporating the environment into the design.

make everything feel welcome

If you add a woven or artificial bug or critter or other accessory, make it look happy and comfortable in the design. Is there a reason why you included this accessory? Give it something to admire or chat or interact with. Is there a way that you can explore nature as a model to mimic? If nature included this piece, how would it naturally occur?

Let the lines of your design lead you to the focal point or point of interest. Keep the attention on the natural beauty.

None of your design elements should ever look as if they are desperately trying to escape.

Yes, your design should always be immaculately crafted (no spilled glue bits, no exposed wire ends, no mechanics unintentionally peeking out, etc.), but that does not mean your design will or should be perfect. Nature is all about imperfection. We can't really craft with nature (or model nature) and strive for perfection at the same time.

Look for the artist's hand in design work. There is exquisite beauty in imperfection.

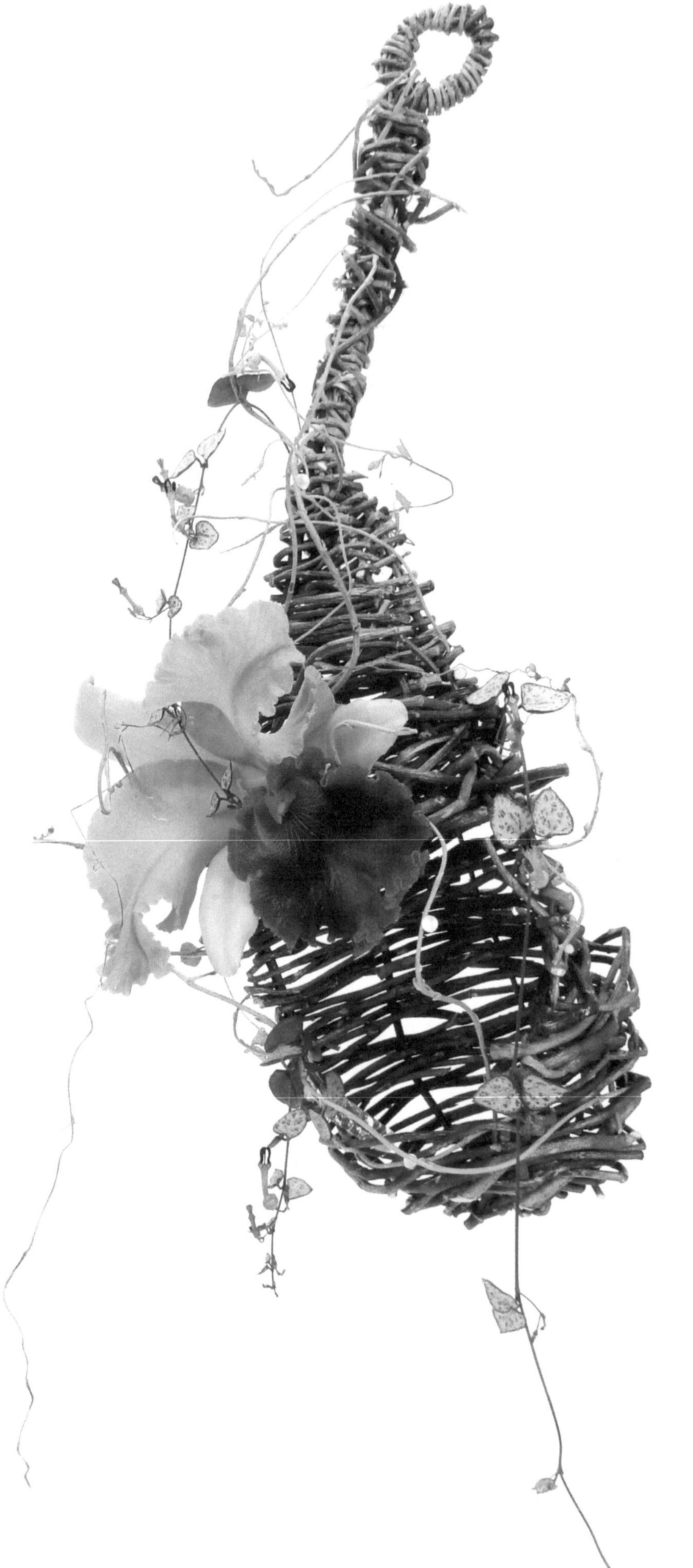

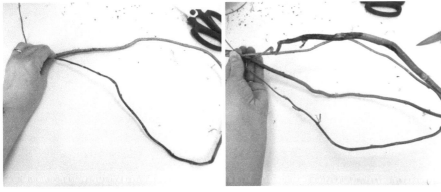

how-to | willow bird nest

Bend a long willow stem into a loop.

Bend another stem to loop inside the first.

Wrap a thin willow stem around the looped stem's ends (be sure to let the longer, thicker side of the stem extend while you use the tip to wrap), and slip the stem end through to secure.

This is the basic nest shape.

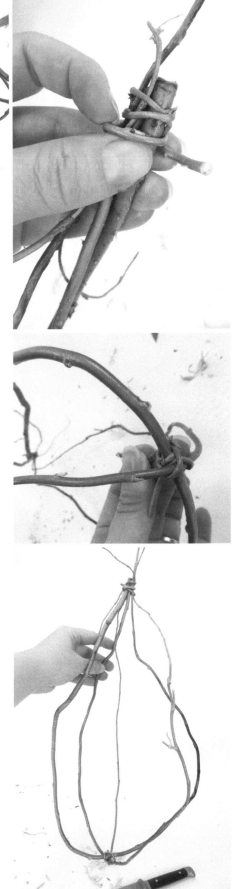

weave and wind the willow bird nest

Secure a thin willow stem where the looped stems cross.

Bend the top stem over and tuck it into the stem you used to connect the loops at the looped end. This creates a fifth stem for you to weave with. Now the nest shape is ready to start weaving.

Press a thin stem into the top where the willow stems are connected and wrap the stem to make sure it is firmly secure and that the stems are all in place.

Press a thin stem in the bottom looped side of the stems. Start weaving the stem in and out, around the stems. I used the basic in-and-out weaving pattern.

Weave the stem in and out, spiraling out around the stems. When you reach the end of a stem, simply add a new stem and continue weaving.

Shape the base of the nest as you spiral out.

Create the opening by looping back the stem at the last willow twig and weaving it back, instead of around. Do the same when you get to the opposite side and continue weaving up, adding stems as you go along.

Do the same at the top, weaving around the stems down to the wider looped side.

Continue to weave all the way around, working your way down to the bottom weaved bit.

Space the stems out to create an opening.

For the loop at the top, loop a willow stem twice and wrap the loop with a thin willow stem. Continue wrapping to cover the entire loop.

Press the looped stems into the willow nest and knot the stems to secure. Add another long stem by pressing it into the wrapped part and wrap the entire top part tightly to secure.

manipulating stems, twigs, and branches

Most stems, twigs, and even sturdier branches can be bent into shapes. It takes practice and more than a bit of patience. The main idea is to slowly manipulate the branch without breaking it. These techniques work on any size branch. Obviously, you will need more force to bend a branch compared to a twig, and you will

need to cushion the stem with the palm of your hand rather than your thumb, or heat the branch with a flame rather than use the heat of your hand, or wire the branch rather than use glue to secure ... but it is still the same basic idea.

Start by snapping a twig. Is it brittle or supple? Brittle branches or twigs should first be soaked in warm water to make them more pliable. Supple branches (such as flowering stems) can be manipulated as-is.

If you want the manipulated branch to keep its shape, it should not be too green. As a rule: if sap runs from the branch when you bend it, it needs to mature or dry out. A moist branch (such as a flowering stem) will not keep the shape you bend it into compared to a slightly dry branch. But a dryer stem will no longer have flowers or foliage.

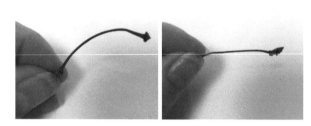

how-to | straighten twigs

Curvy twigs can also be straightened. Hold the stem firmly between your fingers and pull down. Work your way from the top to the bottom as if stretching the twig.

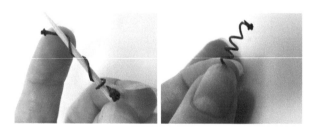

how-to | spiral twigs

Slowly wrap the stem around a dowel stick. Hold the stem in place for a few seconds with your fingers and release.

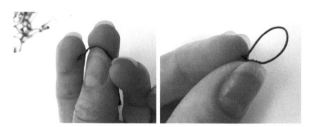

how-to | bend twigs

Gently begin to bend the twig. Cushion the stem with the pad of your finger. Go slowly.

To bend it into a circle, continue to slowly bend the stem from tip to tip. Roll the stem as you go and secure the ends.

how-to

snap a twig at an angle without breaking it

Use your thumb or finger as a supporting cushion. Gently snap the twig. Make sure you do not break the twig. The lower bark should remain intact. This way water will still be transported up the stem to the leaves.

how-to

bend branches and thicker stems

It is also possible to manipulate thicker branches, but you will have to wire and train, weigh it down, or burn it with a flame. But there is a less severe method.

Cut a small wedge. This small wedge will prevent the cut branch from springing back once cut and bend into an angle. Make a deep cut in the branch. Gently bend the branch open.

Insert the wedge into the branch.

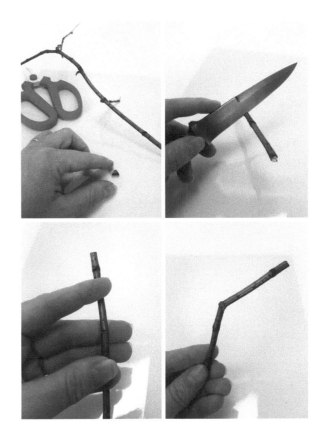

how-to

strip bark

With a sharp knife, cut a slit running down the length of the stem.

Split the stem open and remove the bark.

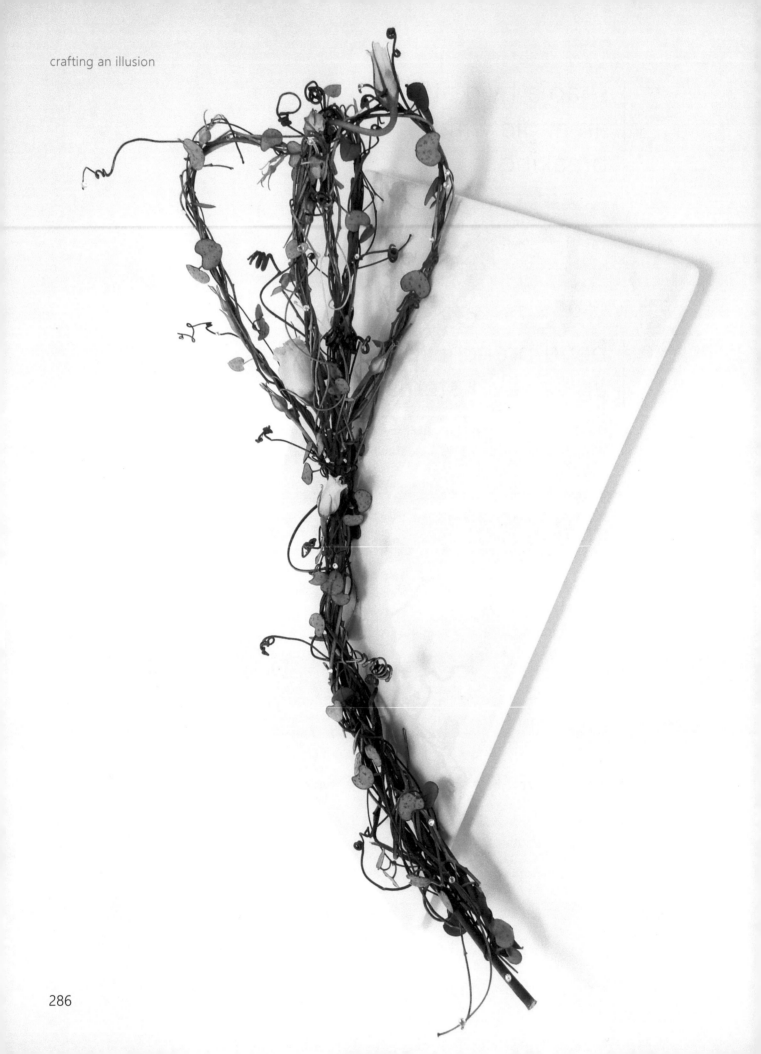

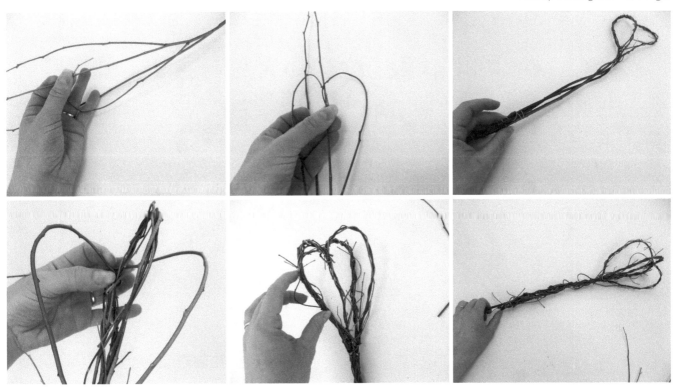

how-to | # eucalyptus heart wand

Manipulate the twigs to create a basic heart shape.

Plait the stems together and weave in a few thinner stems to break up the pattern.

Add two more twigs to craft another heart. Secure it by weaving in more stems around the shape.

how-to | # fresh plant material for the heart wand

Wind the rosary vine around the heart shape. Rosary vine is a succulent and will remain turgid for days. Or you can add a tiny water source by making a water tube from a thin drinking straw.

Nuzzle in the drinking straw water tubes between the twigs so that they are stuck in place. Glue the plant material so that it is in the tiny straws and secured to the heart wand.

Add a few dewdrop crystals and grapevine tendrils.

manipulating grasses

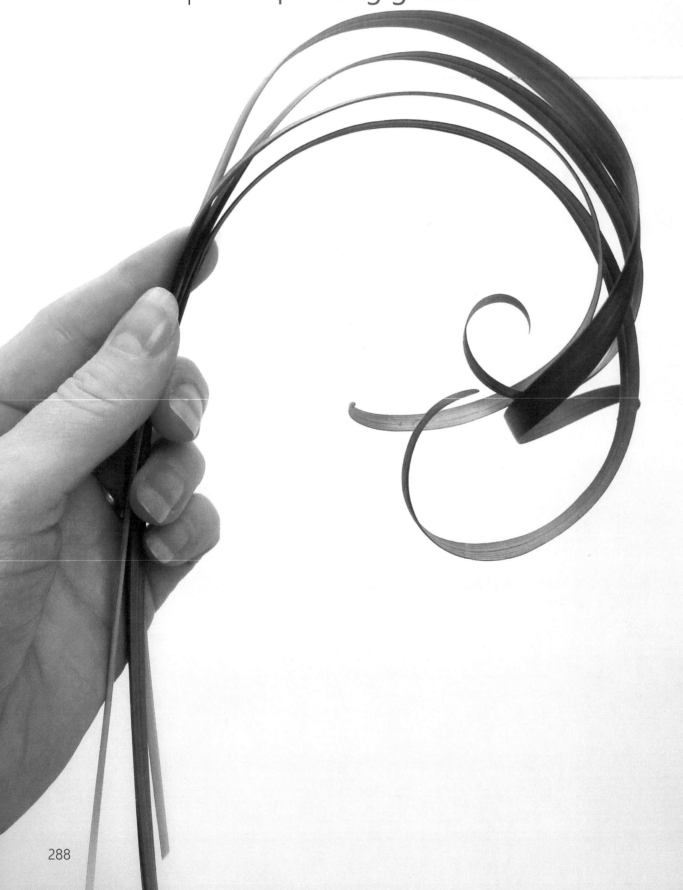

how-to | bend grass at a sharp angle

Cushion the grass with the pad of your thumb to give it support so that it bends and does not break.

Pinch the blade of grass between your finger nail and your thumb.

If you find that you press too hard, use your weaker ring finger, rather than your stronger index finger.

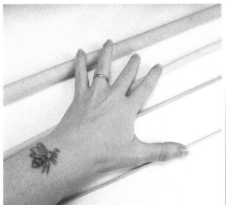

how-to | curl grass

The size of the curl depends on the width of the dowel stick you roll it around. Very similar to curlers.

Roll the blade of grass around the dowel stick. Pull ever so slightly on the grass. The trick is to pull so that the grass is stretched without damaging or ripping it.

Hold the curl on the dowel stick for a few seconds and then release.

Set the grass back into water. The curl is set once the grass is rehydrated.

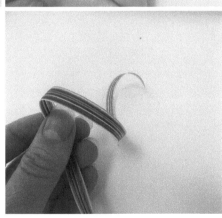

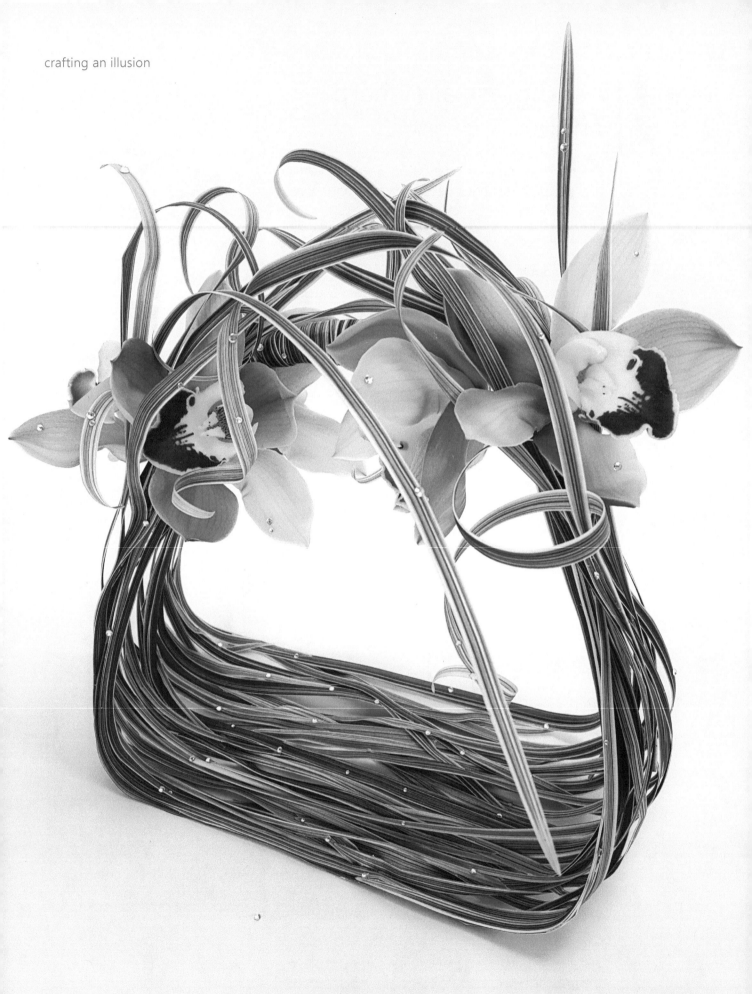

how-to | grass bridal basket

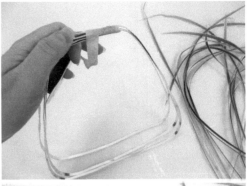

Bend flat wire to create a basket shape. I made mine almost a rounded triangle with a flat top.

Connect the open ends at the top with florist tape. This area will be the handle of the basket.

Space out the wires to create a flat base.

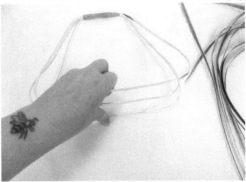

Bind a small bundle of grass to the one side of the basket handle, letting the tips dangle down the side.

Bind another small bundle of grass facing the other way.

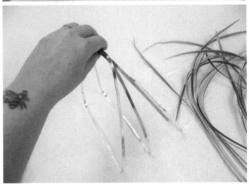

Bend the grass down over the side of the basket and secure to the wire with floral glue.

Repeat on the other side.

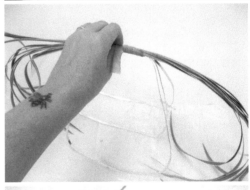

Fold the blades of grass over, and secure them to the bottom of the basket, one strand at a time.

Gather up the stem ends at the handle side of the basket.

Wrap the stems with a blade of grass to create a neat handle.

Glue in a few dangling blades of grass, some snowflake sparkling beads, and the orchids.

Add a few crystals and make sure the basket is comfortable to carry.

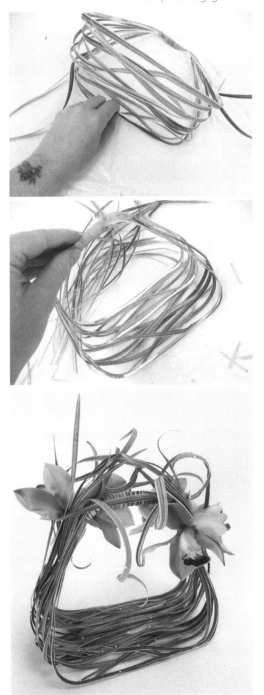

how-to | wrap with grass

Wrap the grass and fold the end piece back into itself to keep it in place.

how-to | cover a vase with a woven grass tangle

Start to weave a few blades of grass. This will form a secure carpet for the vase to rest on.

Rest the small bubble vase on the woven carpet.

Bring a blade of grass over the container and tuck it into the woven bit at the opposite side.

This creates a starting point to tangle the blades of grass.

Randomly weave the grass through the blades in its path so that it folds over the container to weave it into the blades on the other side.

Use the thicker parts of the grass to guide through the tangle.

Keep following the shape of the vase without pulling the grass tight.

Fill the container with water and place the tulips in the container. Add a few blades of grass to curl up and over the tulips.

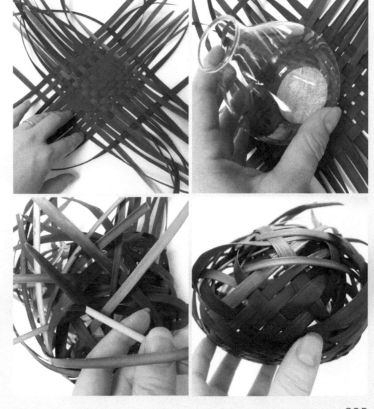

manipulating flowers

how-to | braid tulips

Choose three fully developed tulip stems.

Remove all the foliage from the stems and set the cleaned stems on a flat working surface. Do not set the flowers in water. The stems need to dehydrate to become more flexible for plaiting.

As the cellular structure of the stems weakens, the stems will become more pliable, making it possible to braid the stems together without snapping them. No need to be concerned, because the moment you set the stems in water they will rehydrate and will look fresh for days in the vase.

After about 30 minutes, the stem will flop over when you pick it up. Carefully watch the flowers, though. You want the stem to be pliable, but there should be no visible sign of

stress on the flower petals.

Place the stems on a working surface to match in length. Cut to be exactly the same size. Look carefully at the flower head. Each flower is closed in two crowns and three perianth petals.

Carefully remove two petals from the first tulip. This opens up the cup.

Carefully remove two petals from a second tulip to open up that flower cup.

Cut or pinch the stamen and pistil away from the stem to create a flat surface. Do the same with the other open cup tulip.

Place a tiny drop of glue on the wound. This not only seals the wound, preventing further moisture loss, but also keeps the flower cups in place.

Slip the full tulip into the tulip with the open cup. Slip those two tulips into the second open cup of the flower head.

The three tulip flower heads are now connected and ready to be braided together.

Carefully start to braid the stems together. Set them aside for a few more minutes if the stems start to snap, but they should be quite dehydrated by now and fairly easy to braid. Move down the length of the stem and braid as you go along.

Give each stem a fresh cut, just above the white area on the stem, at an angle, to increase the surface that will be exposed to water.

Place the stems into water to recondition.

| how-to | # reflex petals |

Tulip petals can be opened or reflexed to create a fuller bloom.

Remove the tulips from water for a half an hour to slightly dehydrate.

Gently place your finger on the thicker part of the petal where it is connected to the stem and pop the petal backward to open.

If the petal starts to tear, leave it for a few minutes more to dehydrate. This works best on tulips in full bud (about four days old).

Carefully reflex the next petal, working your way around the flower, gently bending each petal open. Set them back in water to fully hydrate.

| how-to | # deliberately create a wound to slow down the growth of tulips |

The stems will continue to twist and turn in your design and grow about the length of their flower heads every day. It is always best to design with this unpredictable growth pattern in mind. Sometimes when you make a small design or for competition or bridal work, you want to minimize growth. The best way to do this is to divert their energy.

With a corsage pin, prick a wound through the stem of the tulip, below the base of the flower head. This will create a wound, and the tulip will focus on sealing the wound rather than on growth.

The tulip will still grow slightly, but not nearly enough to make the design unpredictable.

how-to | # straighten tulip stems

Wrap the bunch of flowers in brown paper and place them in fresh water to condition overnight. As the stems take up water, they become straight.

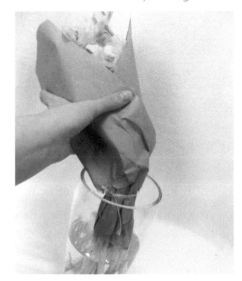

how-to | # curve calla lilies

Let the calla lilies rest out of water for about 30 minutes to slightly dehydrate. Gently massage the stem to curve.

Follow the flower's natural curve or curve only sections to create an elegant crescent or a curve at the tip of the stem. Place the stem back into water and condition as normal. The stem will become firm, and the curve will remain.

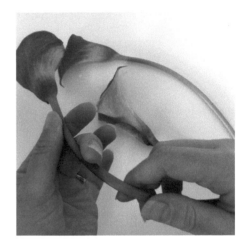

how-to | # minimize negative geotropism

The top few buds of gladioli always curve up and away from gravity. This creates an elegant line, but sometimes you need the stem to remain straight, especially in a horizontal design. To minimize the negative geotropism in flowers such as gladioli, nip away the tip most unopened bud.

how-to | # tap an iris open

Gently tap the closed iris bud on your finger to pop it open.

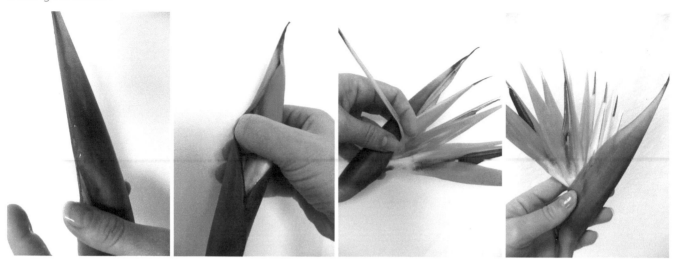

how-to | open strelitzias

If you want completely unblemished petals, purchase the bird of paradise flowers when the petals are still hidden in the spathe, and carefully coax them open. The flowers will not open by themselves once cut.

Pour warm water in a tub or bowl. It should be deep enough to soak the flower heads. Rest your hand in the water. If the water feels hot or cold, you need to adjust it. It should be body temperature.

Soak the flower heads for 20 minutes to hydrate and plump up the petals. Petals that are fully hydrated (and at room temperature) are less likely to bruise when handled a bit roughly, and it will also be easier to reach in and open a full bloom.

Soak the flower head (or sheath or spathe) in water and gently separate the seam of the spathe.

Slip your thumb into the bud.

Slide your finger below all the petals right to the front of the spathe to release the entire bloom from the sheath or spathe.

Rinse away any gel-like, sticky sap that runs from the flower in clean water. Carefully separate and fan out all the petals.

The thin, ivory-coloured petals are guard petals. These can either be kept if they will enhance your design or remove them by tucking them out. Tearing out these guard petals makes it easier to fully open the entire bloom.

Coax the flowers to fan out. Tuck any undeveloped petals back into the spathe if you do not want them to show.

When the entire flower is fanned open, give the stem two cuts (into a point) to expose it to as much water as possible. Set it back into water to hydrate.

how-to | open lilies faster

Lilies open faster in warm and humid environments.

To open the flowers, you can roll the petals to loosen them. This only works with a well-developed bud that is already the colour that it will be when it is open.

Gently roll the lily between your fingers or between the palms of your hands until the petals start to pop open. Carefully peel the petals open.

how-to | keep flowers in bud for longer

Dip or paint the bud with egg white to prevent it from opening. This will also work with any pod-shaped flowers, such as tulips.

how-to | disk floret

Pick away the petals of chrysanthemums or sunflowers to expose the disk floret.

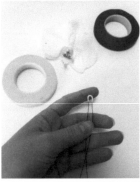

how-to | wire and tape flowers and foliage

Wiring flowers gives them a flexible wire and taped stem to manipulate into the exact position you want.

The florist tape becomes tacky when handled. Make sure you stretch the tape as you go along so that it adheres.

Match the colour of the tape and new wire stem to the natural flower stem.

With orchids that get wired through the flower in a way that it is seen, first match the colour of the tape to the flower where it will be visible and wrap only a bit of wire. In this case it can either be yellow or white. Fold the wire into a hairpin.

Catch it over the throat of the orchid without piercing the petals.

Then tape the rest of the wire to match the stem.

You can also air-tape flowers by taping without the wire for support for a drape stem.

how-to | # a secret water source for wired flowers

Flowers such as orchids are slow drinkers. Even the smallest amount of water can make a huge difference in the quality of these flowers. This can extend the life of a design by days.

Cut a drinking straw into a small section. Plug one side with hot glue and fill the straw with water.

Slip the straw over the tiny flower stem. Even if held upside down, the water stays in the tiny straw.

Wire the flower as you normally would, then wrap the wire around the straw.

Start to tape the stem just above the straw. Tape over the opening and cover the straw. Tape down the wire to create the wire stem.

The stem might be a little more bulky than normal, but on a hot day it is worth the trouble to keep body flowers from wilting.

If you use the flower for a corsage, make sure not to press the pin through the straw or use a corsage magnet rather than a pin.

manipulating leaves, petals and foliage

how-to | cone-shaped autumn leaves

Gather a wide variety (in shape, type, and colour) of autumn leaves to create a full and interesting rosette. Use the smaller ones for the first three rows, the ones with the longest stems for the gap fillers, and the largest leaves to shape the inside circles.

Cut a large cardboard circle.

To start the pattern, roll the first batch of autumn leaves into cone shapes and glue the leaves to the outer edge of the cardboard. Glue leaves all the way around.

Start on a second row of leaves, just inside the first row and another inside that.

The leaves will shrink as they dry, leaving a few gaps. Fill in the gaps with fresh leaves and set aside to dry.

Place the rosette on a chalice-shaped vase. Glue in twigs and weave them around the rosette to conceal the cardboard edge.

Glue in a few water tubes to keep the fresh plant material hydrated.

how-to | foliage roses

I used to make baskets full of these when I was a little girl. We had a big yellow mimosa tree, and I used to spear my roses onto the tree, pretending I was the fairy responsible for bringing blossoms.

Begin your rose by rolling a middle bud. Secure it with wire, which will also become the stem.

I prefer to roll all my petals in advance. Roll the top, thin part of the leaf, then roll the two sides of the leaf, creating three rolled sides. Set aside.

Start adding the leaves from small to big.

This works best if the leaves are slightly dehydrated but not yet dry. I prefer to collect the leaves first thing in the morning.

Continue adding petals to create a nice, full-shaped rose.

Clutch and wrap a wire around the stem ends to tie the leaves together.

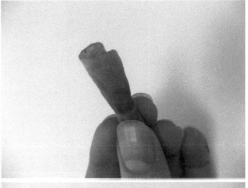

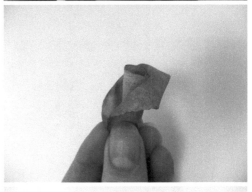

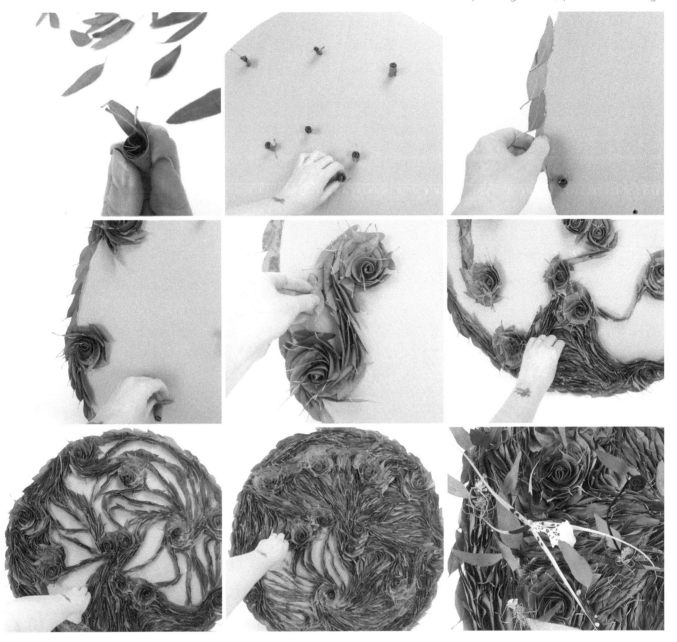

how-to | eucalyptus leaf swirl

My entire swirl is made by gluing the leaves in a lengthwise position.

Roll a few leaves to create rosettes and glue them randomly to a large cardboard circle.

Glue leaves around the edge of the cardboard to set the pattern of the swirl.

Start gluing a few swirls around the rosettes.

Fill in the swirl pattern by extending the rosettes and letting them flow in with the leaves glued to the edges.

Glue in a few sticks and water tubes for the fresh orchids.

how-to | peg leaf angles

Carefully fold the leaves into blocks and pin them into place with split bamboo sections.

Overlap the leaves' ends so that they are secure.

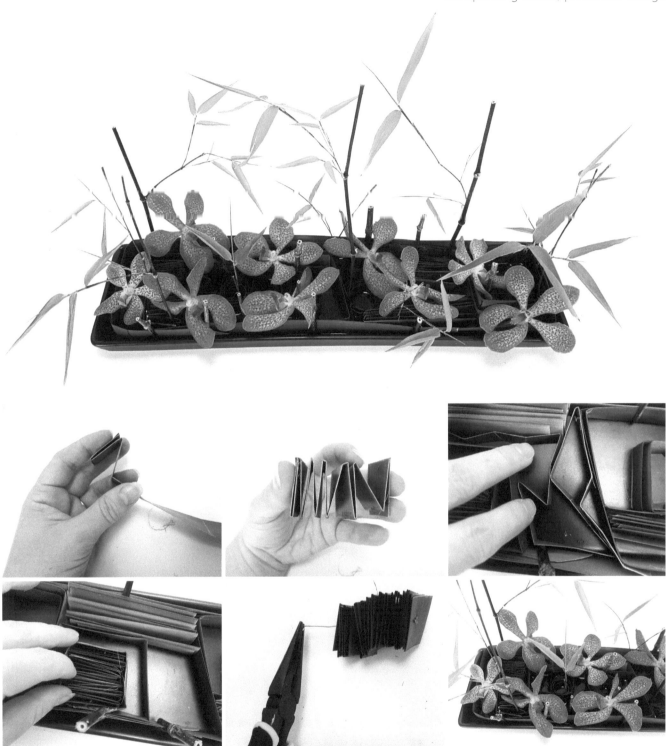

how-to | fold a zig zag

For an unpredictable zigzag, simply place the folded leaves in the container and let them settle at random angles.

To keep the zigzag in place, either place it in a space exactly the same size as the zigzag so that it kicks against the side to stay in place, or press a wire through the zigzag to keep it together.

inspired by | a ladder

inspiration

*"crafting with nature is about creating
beauty and joy, and creativity,
with that which already are all those things.
it is therefore not possible
to totally suck at it."*

We have packed our tools and practiced our techniques. We have explored how to make those techniques our own. In this chapter and the next, let's look at how we know and agree on what is meant in our designs.

First, we'll look at the inspirations behind the concepts: our shared medium (nature), with which we develop a successful concept with appropriate techniques; and our flower-arranging traditions, which give us the vocabulary to understand and communicate with each other through our designs.

Then, in the next chapter, we'll look at how we respond to these inspirations (and a few more ideas) through personal exploration, to interpret our own art, creating a clear, concise, and meaningful expression of the theme, brief, or idea.

How do we tell each other stories in the language of flowers so that we all understand?

When a floral artist enters a competition, he receives a schedule that clearly stipulates which theme should be interpreted. The artist then prepares for the competition by finding the inspiration behind what is stipulated in the schedule and then interprets this theme to make it his own.

The same process occurs for a client brief, design specification, or a personal vision. Sympathy flowers convey a message of support for loss. Clear and concise. If you want to create a design celebrating spring, you use happy, youthful elements. Even the simplest corsage design is loaded with symbolic value.

inspired by

as light as snow

We say we are inspired when we receive a schedule, a brief, find a beautiful flower or image and something about this sparks our imagination and we have an artistic impulse to create. By clearly understanding why or what is meant or intended by this bit of inspiration we gain deeper insight into what exactly is expected of us when we develop a concept that will become a meaningful expression of emotion.

Developing a concept always starts with exploring what you already know. These are your constraints, limits or rules that you will have to work with. These are also your inspiration kick-starters. Why are you doing this? What is it you want to do? What is asked of you? It could be a wedding bouquet, something pretty for next to your bed or a fantastical design for a competition. The answers to these questions provide a fundamental guideline to what you need to develop.

nature

As a floral designer or floral artist, it is safe to assume that you are required to, or want to, craft with nature. Most competition schedules will clearly stipulate that some materials are forbidden. We will find the words, "Fresh flowers and plant material must predominate" somewhere in the rules. Whatever we are required to (or desire to) create will be made up primarily of plant material. Your plant material should always tell your story. Plants are the focal point of your concept.

Our greatest source of inspiration when developing a concept will therefore always be nature.

What plant material would you like to use? Think of different situations and the plant material you would naturally choose to represent them. What flowers scream happiness to you? Or hope, gratitude, love, or sorrow? How will your flower choices affect your design?

inspired by | nature

how-to | sink a hidden water source into driftwood

Measure your drill bit against the water tube. It should be an exact fit so that the tube is snug and supported in the hole.

Drill a hole in the wood and sink the tube into the hole.

Fill with water and add your fresh design elements.

inspired by

what is already there

how-to | design a ring around a monster

This design is inspired by the natural holes in the monstera leaf.

Make a lightweight ring of cane and thread it through two holes in the monstera leaf.

Glue the ring with wood glue at the back.

I used succulents to complete my design because they do not require a water source. Wrap the rosary vines loosely around the cane.

Fill in the spaces between the heart-shaped leaves with snipped kalanchoe. Add a few dewdrop crystals and some grape tendrils for contrast.

The kalanchoe flowers last for about a week in a design like this.

technique

For me, the next step in finding inspiration is technique. You are making something that does not yet exist, and you must apply some how-to to accomplish that challenge.

Every time we craft something, our skills are tested in one way or another. We create to see if we can make whatever we are creating. This can be a great source of inspiration or a driving force behind developing a concept.

I rarely reach for a floral design image or conduct an internet search for inspiration for my concepts. I find great inspiration in figuring out how to make something. I have always been playing with flowers. As a little girl, I would spend hours weaving and building fairy castles from twigs and petals. I still use the techniques I made up then. Those are my effortless, go-to techniques. They are as much a part of me as my name. These basics are ideal for developing concepts because I can expand on them on demand, even under pressure.

You need to pay attention to the use of techniques when developing your composition. If it is for an event or a competition, you need to consider how long the plant material should last. Is the way that you plan to construct your design stable—even curious-onlooker stable? Is this the best technique, the most appropriate for what you were asked to do? How will your design choices, design variety, budget, and location affect the techniques you choose to use? Every technique is important, even the simple ones. All are part of what inspire your concept.

inspired by

the shape of a vase

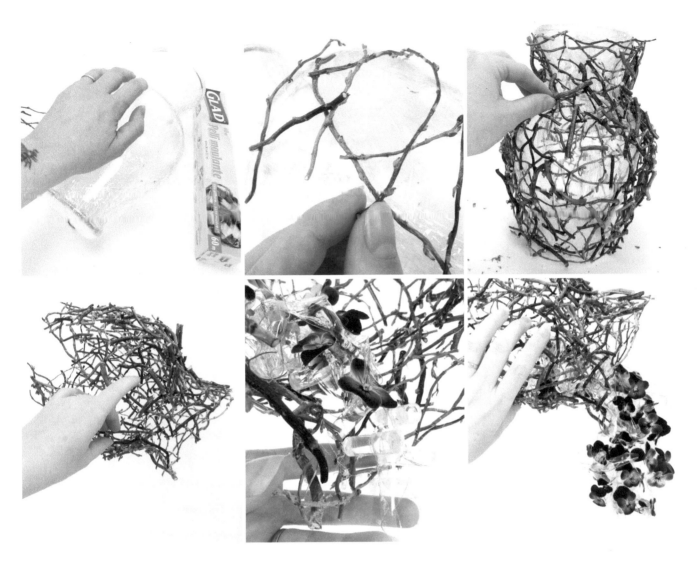

how-to | glue twig snippets into a vase shape

Cover a glass vase with plastic wrap and smooth it down.

Glue twig snippets to closely follow the shape. Curve the snippets around the vase, leaving a gap so that you can remove the twig-vase from the glass-vase.

Connect the two halves at one side with additional twig snippets. Wiggle the twigs to make sure the shape is secure. Add twigs or glue down twigs where needed.

Glue twigs to create the base of the vase shape and fit it to the twig armature to make sure it is the right size. Add twigs if necessary. Do not glue it down yet so that it is easier to design the flowers in the vase part of the armature.

I made the clear part of the armature by melting snipped plastic soda bottles into shapes with warm water. Build up the armature and glue the test tubes to fit into the plastic shapes.

Glue in bits of grass so that it looks like grass is tumbling from the snippet vase.

inspired by | a blissful
snowman

tradition ... in an original way

The third inspiration behind developing your concept can be found in language. Read and understand the requirements. Explore the language in our floral design traditions.

The word *tradition* is derived from *tradere* or *traderer*, literally meaning "to give for safekeeping." I love that. It fits my design philosophy.

We are given our floral design traditions to keep them safe. Safe does not mean locking them in a vault so that they become dated and irrelevant. Safe means respectfully revitalizing our craft form so that these traditions can continue to grow and flourish with new life in our contemporary design environment.

Whether it is a style of floristry (such as Ikebana, English Country Garden, European, or High Style American...) or the design styles (such as a Biedermeier, Hogarth curve, or a Floral Object...) or techniques (such as weaving, wrapping, or knotting...), well, anything we have inherited, our work will, at some point, be described in the language of our tradition, and you will need to interpret that language or recognize it as an inspiration. Language is always going to play a role in the concept of floral design. The traditions of the craft is our dictionary.

Because we are creating rather than recreating or reproducing, we will also be required to do so with distinction. If your concept ventures too far from the traditional description, you risk being misunderstood and alienating the judge, onlooker, or recipient of your work (which is perfectly fine if that is your intention as an artist, of course). If your concept is too familiar (once again, which is perfectly fine if you are an artist specializing in perfecting traditional styles), you run the risk of being misunderstood and considered boring. Most of us work somewhere in the middle. Yes, you the artist are expected to create a new-familiar. Designing for Christmas is a great example of this: people want something new with just a hint of nostalgia.

A good way to revisit tradition in your work is to consider whether or not you favour traditional associations. Do you always design with carnations for Mother's Day or roses on Valentine's Day?

Or do you lean to a more contemporary approach that favours personal preference?

How do you feel about variety in forms and styles in contemporary designs? For example, wreaths are no longer assumed to be round. What is your personal reaction to a non-round wreath?

inspired by

letting it go

Tutorials - Woven lily gra...

http://www.christinedebeer.ca/tutorials/woven-lily-grass-pa

MY CREATIVE WORKBOOK

Christine de Beer Floral Lifestyle Design

n lily grass parachute armature

y 2016 ☺☺☺☺☺☺☺☺... click to send Christine a smile

of grass in a horizontal position on a flat working surface

nore detailed instructions on how to weave with foliage

Christine de Beer
Floral Lifestyle Design

Christine de Beer
Floral Lifestyle Design

christine@christinedebeer.ca
www.christinedebeer.ca

I often go back to the traditional to find the new. While my work is thoroughly contemporary, I use ancient, cultural and traditional techniques in my contemporary concepts. But part of finding the new is letting go of the old.

When revisiting tradition for inspiration as you design new concepts, it is important to have some strategy to let go of some of the old ideas so that you do not find yourself stuck, merely doing things like you have always done them.

For me, this is turning the concept into art. Actually completing the project, or taking part in the competition. Even for the concepts that just pop into my head when I am inspired by something that I read or by a flower I buy. I find crafting the art and sharing it with my flower friends help me to stay open to new inspiration. When I place a new design on the *My Creative Workbook* website with the design tutorials, I feel a sense of " been there and done that," and I can move on to the next creative thought. Of course, I do have my favourites that I revisit.

I find that working, actually doing the designs, opens up the flow to more ideas. If I am working, my next idea lines up in time for me to create it. If I get stuck on a design and need more time to finish it (for instance, when I am working on a few demonstration designs that explore a similar theme or a competition design that takes a few months to prepare for), a flood of design ideas get stuck in my imagination. Then the natural flow of ideas slows down or stops, and I have to go through a period of doing some work to get this flow going again after the design, that caused the holdup in the first place, is complete. Sometimes it helps to sketch out ideas that occur to me to keep the creative energy going. Most of the time in that period of re-starting the creative flow, that is when I will revisit my favourite ideas and see how I can improve or reinterpret them. The important thing is to keep working. Not every design is going to be a fantastic, clear interpretation of your vision. Do the work anyway. Be willing to fail. Make the art anyway.

I am the world's worst procrastinator. Just not in the way that you might think. I simply can not do it.

I want to do things right away. While my enthusiasm is high and the idea is fresh in my mind. This is when inspiration burst into full blossom, and my energy levels spike.

This method of working is not always ideal for a floral designer because we can obviously not add fresh plant material far in advance of an event. I have learned to compensate by using perfect-for-do-ahead-of-time-dried-plant-material as my basic armature. This work-around gives me plenty of time to stare at, dream about, and visualize on how to expand my original idea. I place it in its project tray and then add fresh plant material as it becomes appropriate.

The important thing is to find solutions that keep your inspiration flowing.

inspired by

a dream catcher

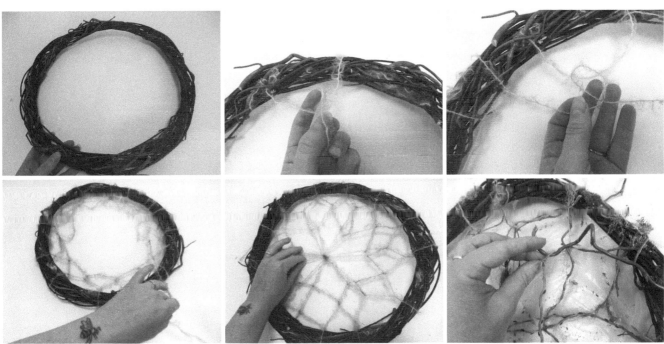

how-to | craft an overgrown willow dream catcher

Weave a strong wreath. Soften the overall look of the wreath by filling the gaps with wool.

Tie wool to the wreath and secure with a knot. Create a loop in the wool by loosely wrapping the wool around the wreath. I measured the loop to be about four finger widths away.

Move around the wreath, creating wool loops.

Moving inward, start a second row of loops, this time looping the wool around the middle of the first row of loops.

Add loops all the way around the wreath. Pull the loops to the middle point of the wreath. I moved this gathering point slightly off-center, to shift the focal point and make my design look more natural. Secure the loops with a knot and glue in clumps of moss.

Weave in thin willow stems following the wool pattern. Gently wrap each stem around the wool to cover the entire armature. Let the stems point inward, toward the focal point. This creates the impression that the stems grow from the wreath into the design.

Double up on some of the sections to create a natural feel.

Place tiny test tubes as a water source for the fresh flowers and glue in the dried hydrangea florets.

how-to | tabletop eucalyptus lei

Thread eucalyptus leaves to create a long garland.

Tie the ends to secure.

Display the lei on a clear container.

how-to | add fresh plant material

If you use flowers with longer stems, you can fill the container with water and place the stems in that container to keep them hydrated.

I wanted my vase base clear to emphasize the shape of the lei, so I nuzzled water tubes between the leaves to keep the flowers hydrated.

inspired by

ballet slippers

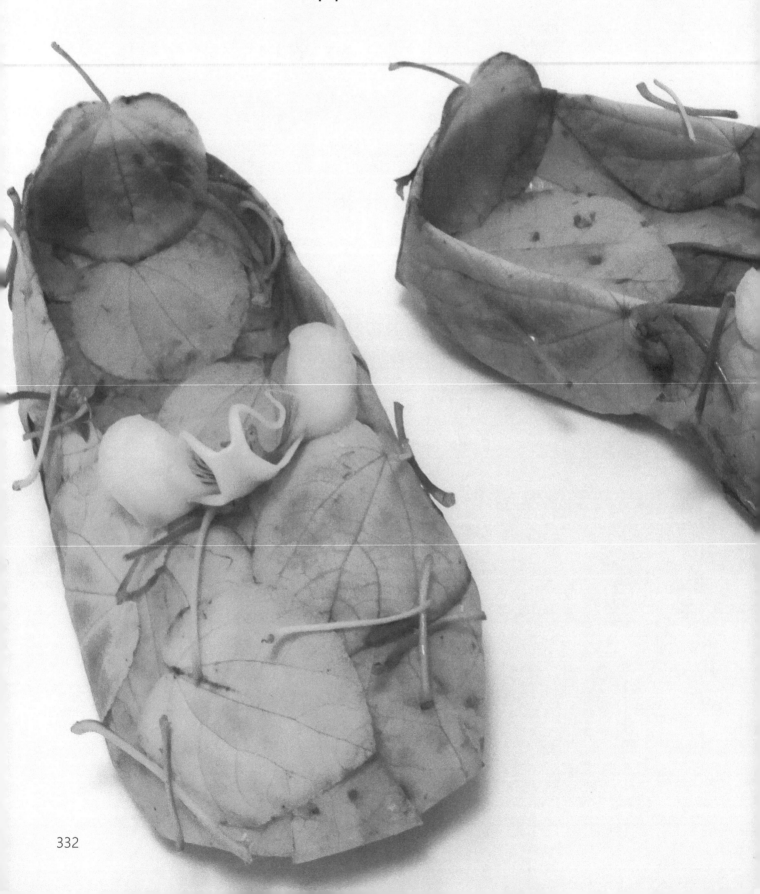

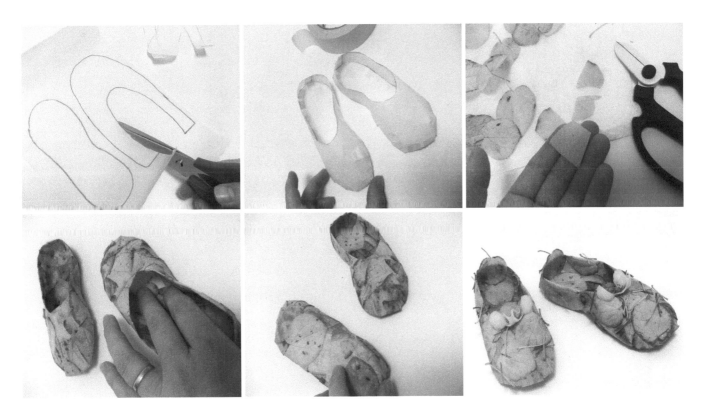

how-to | craft slippers from autumn leaves

Draw the slipper pattern on thin paper.

Cut out the ballet slipper pattern.

Place the two slipper soles down on a working surface.

Tape the upper to the sole following the contours with a few strips of masking tape.

Wash and dry a few autumn leaves.

Cut the stems from the leaves and set aside. Cut a few of the leaves in irregular blocks.

Glue the fall leaves to the paper slipper.

Overlap the leaves so that they will cover the paper as they dry and shrink.

Completely cover the paper slipper with fall leaves so that it can be picked up and viewed from all angles.

Smooth down the edges of the leaves to lie flat.

Reach deep into the slipper toe and cover the inside sole.

Flip the slipper over and cover the sole.

Glue on the leaf stems to add texture and decorate with flowers.

glue a heart-shaped armature

Draw a heart shape on paper.

Match a few sprouting spring twigs to follow the shape of the heart. Carefully glue in twigs to offer support.

As a rule of thumb, I glue each twig, that will be a connection, in three places to create a really strong armature.

Glue the twig heart onto a sprouting twig and place it at an angle in a container filled with water.

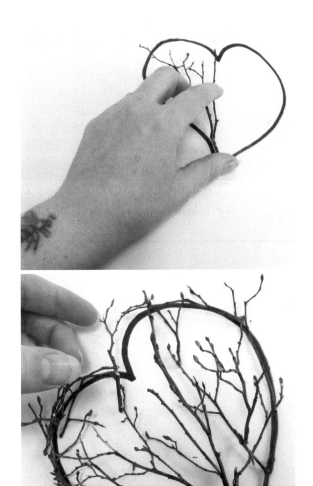

inspired by

| filigree jewelry

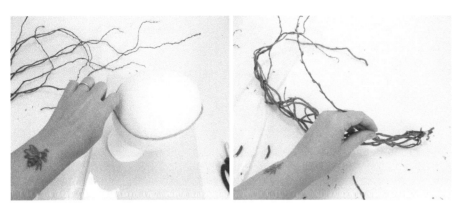

how-to | weave a willow crown

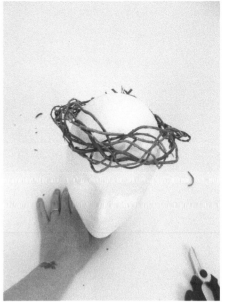

Use a length of ribbon to measure the width of the person's head to custom-design the crown. This way you can have the measurements ahead of time and start weaving the fresh plant material just before it is needed.

Measure out the fresh and pliable willow stems. Gather the stems and gently manipulate them by bending them down the length of the stem. This way you make the stems more pliable so that you can weave them without snapping the stems. Secure the stems at one end with an elastic band. The band will be removed eventually, but securing them makes it easier to weave the stems. Gently plait and weave the stems into a long tangle.

Measure the ribbon against the plaited willow to see if it is long enough.

Remove the elastic band and weave the two ends together to connect the willow crown.

Fit the crown and make adjustments if necessary.

Glue in the flowers, moss, and sparkling beads.

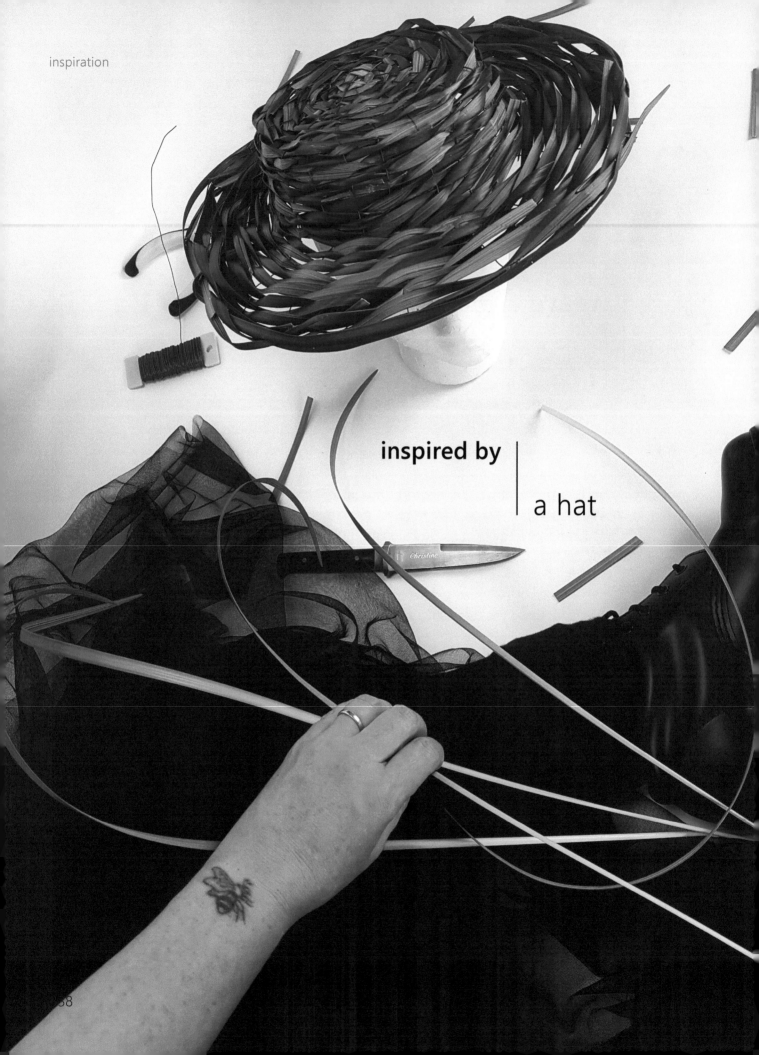

inspired by | a hat

weave a grass hat

This is the basic pattern used to weave a hat. It is actually very easy to weave. If you get the first strand (or garland) right, it is basic weaving until the hat is the size you need.

Measure the wires to fit the size of the hat. You will need eight short wires and one long garland of lily grass to weave with. Make the garland by gluing blades of grass into a continuous length.

Work on a flat surface to get the weave started. We start at the bowl of the hat. Work in pairs and lay the first two pieces on your working surface.

Cross the next two strands over the first two. Weave in two more pairs of strands. The second pair goes over the first but under the pair below. The pair next to the first goes under and the pair below over.

Start weaving in the long grass garland. Place the garland parallel to the four horizontal wires. The end of the garland should be as long as the horizontal wire on the left side so that it becomes a fifth horizontal strand on that side.

Bend the long side of the garland down to start the spiral weave. First weave the long garland through the middle garlands in couples.

Weave the garland over the first two and under the next two strands. Give it a twist and continue this weaving pattern around the strands. Include the new strand that was created with the garland.

Weave another spiral, twisting the grass as you make a turn in the spiral, holding all the wires in place with grass.

Space out the strands to all the sides to radiate out.

Weave the garland of grass over or under every wire, following the basic weaving pattern.

Continue weaving the garland grass to create the bowl of the hat.

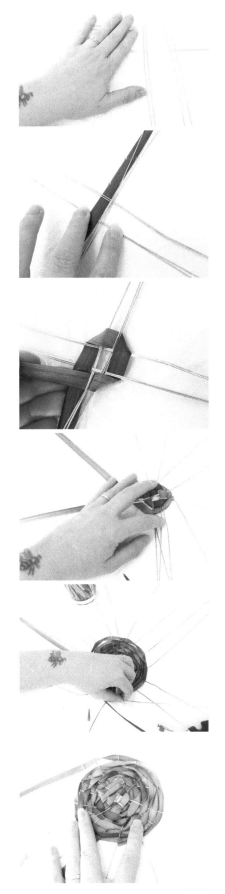

Bend the wires up.

Weave the sides of the bowl, giving the grass a twist at every turn.

Weave around and around, creating the bowl of the hat.

When you have a neat bowl, bend the strands down and straight out to create the brim.

Move all the way around, spacing out the strands to radiate.

Flip the design around so that the brim is flat and resting on your working surface.

Continue the weaving pattern, moving around the brim, twisting the grass at every wire.

Continue the weaving pattern, moving around the brim.

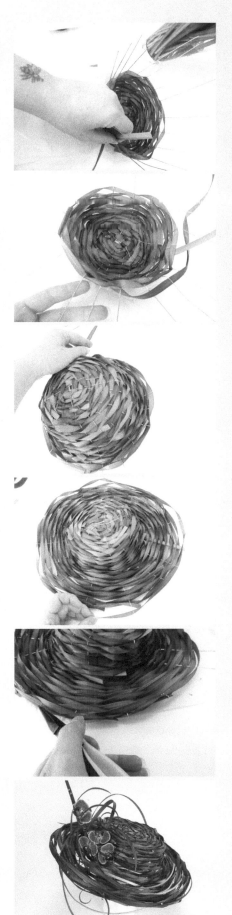

Bend the wires over with pliers.

Weave another strand around the brim of the hat to secure and hide the wire ends.

Glue in the floral details.

inspired by

a net

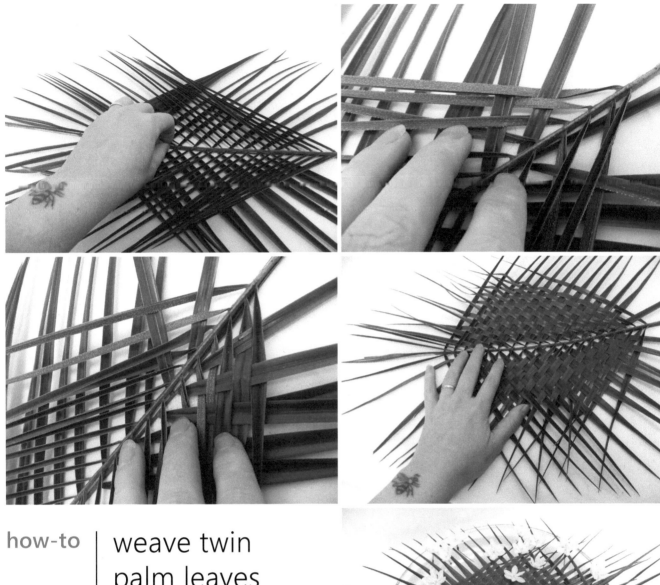

how-to | weave twin palm leaves

Choose two palm leaves that are identical in size for the weave. Place one palm leaf on the other so that both stems face out to the opposite sides.

Start to weave the leaves.

Open up and smooth the leaf as you weave.

Smooth the spine of the leaf so that it lies flat.

Wiggle each leaf to create a tight and neat weave.

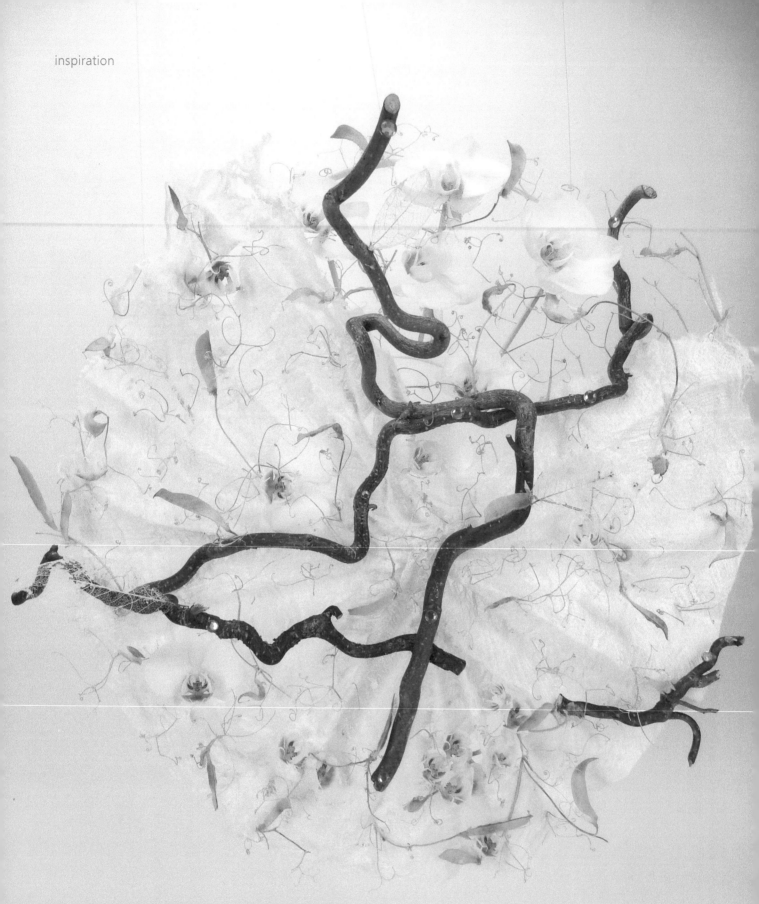

inspired by

a paper fan

how-to | fanned-out bleached mulberry bark armature

Place a mulberry sheet flat on a working surface.

Decide how wide you want the concertina folds to be.

Fold over the first strip of bleached mulberry in the width you want the creases to be.

Fold the next strip under in the same width. The strip thereafter gets folded over and then the next under. Finish folding the entire sheet.

Connect the folds on the sheet at the bottom with a butterfly clip and glue to secure.

Fold another fan. Glue to connect. I left a gap to showcase the orchids at the top.

Craft a basic structure from cane to support the fan armature. Glue the armature to the cane and add the floral details.

inspired by | luxury

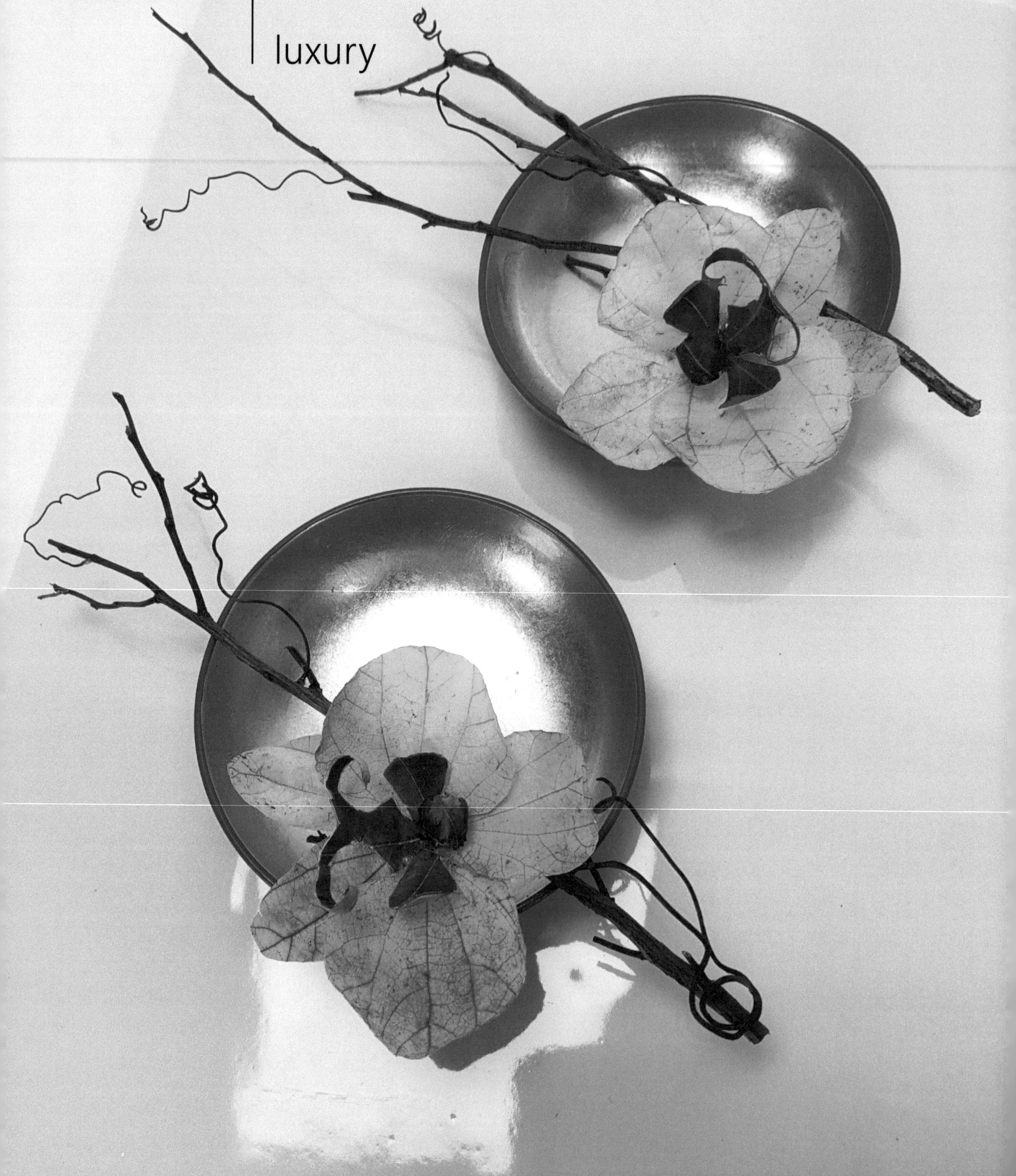

| # make a phalaenopsis orchid from autumn leaves

Cut the two petals from a fall leaf.

Cut the sepals.

Cut the stigma and lobe from a larger leaf.

Manipulate the leaves to curve them.

Glue the pieces together to shape the orchid.

Wrap a berry with an autumn leaf and glue it into position.

Curve the flower by rolling it over a bamboo skewer.

inspired by | a cage

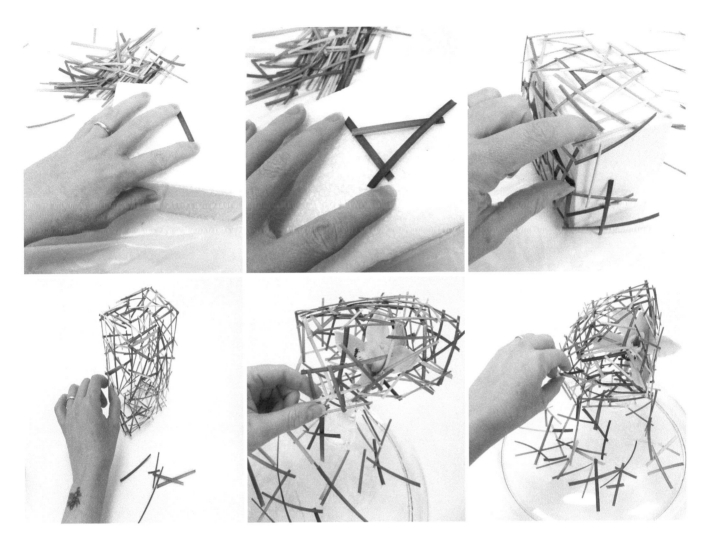

how-to | glue a cage

Glue grass snippets around a Styrofoam shape.

Make sure you glue the snippets to the other snippets and not to the foam.

Glue each snippet in such a way that it connects with the other snippets in at least three points.

Leave one side open to pull the grass block away from the shape.

Place over a small container. Balance the block on the container and place the flower.

Finish the design by gluing the side that was left open closed with grass snippets.

Add a few tumbling snippets to the design.

inspired by

a ball

how-to

wild gap basket

Weave a small wreath.

Wiggle a stem through the wreath to loop toward the bottom to create the shape of the basket.

Weave in a few more stems to create a sturdy basket.

how-to

half a sphere lid

I used a glass ball vase to give me the basic shape for the lid.

Bend pliable stems to follow the shape of the vase and secure with painter's tape.

Set the lid aside for the twigs to dry.

Add a few drops of glue to make sure it keeps its shape before removing the painter's tape and setting it over the basket design.

351

inspired by | a piano

how-to | line stems in a row

Cut stems the width of your container. I used off-cut pieces of stems I used in other designs. The burgundy is fiddlehead fern stems, and the green is calla lily stems.

Thread the stems with a thin wire at both ends to line up.

Continue to add stems the length of your container. I did not follow a colour pattern, but you can if you prefer.

Place the stems on the container and bend the wire over at both ends to secure. Cut the wire short where needed.

Space out the stems. Fill the container with water and add the fresh floral material.

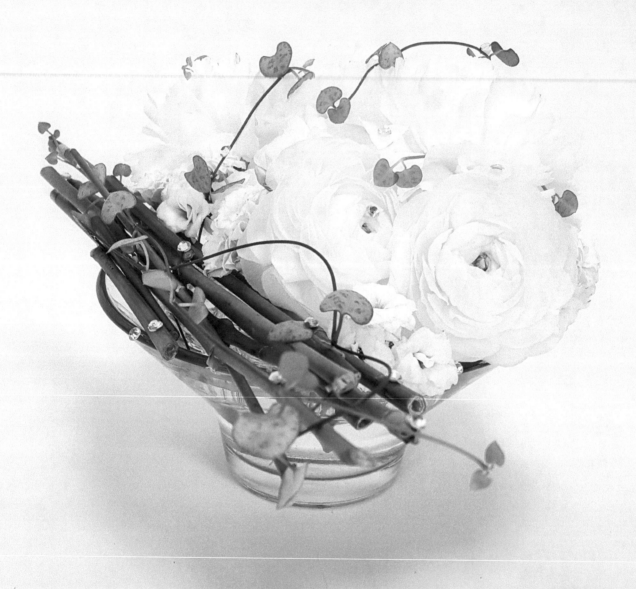

design note | ## as a rule of thumb

If I feel the need to explain my interpretation, I am on the wrong path. Your message should be self-explanatory to the point of obvious.

Simplicity in the message. Creativity in the execution. Perfection in the craftsmanship.

say it in flowers

"*flowers are feelings made visible*"

It is easier to explore what it is you want to say once you understand the inspiration behind your design concept.

Designing with flowers is telling a story. The flowers you pick are the words. The art of arranging is adding meaning. The way you do it is your style. Above all this is what floral art is about, and what this chapter is about. Floral artists speak Flowers. In other words, floral artists find a respectful way to explore, expand, and interpret, and ultimately tell a story in the form of a carefully constructed illusion.

It is a rare talent to always be able to say exactly the right thing at the right time. Even more so, it is difficult to say the right thing in sad or tragic circumstances or when you are under stress. Fortunately, even the humblest flower possesses that talent. Flowers speak the words we wish we could, and it is our task as floral designers to make it easy for anyone, by looking at our designs, to interpret, understand, and experience the message on an emotional level.

We have been speaking in flowers for a long time. In Victorian times, people were much more restrained in what was socially acceptable to communicate. So they quite ingeniously developed a secret language to send their messages by types, colours, maturity, and method of delivering flowers. Even the way flowers were received or accepted influenced the meaning of the message.

The language of flowers (Floriography) is hugely culture dependent. For instance, in Japan it is called Hanakotoba. Floriography interprets a yellow tulip as: there is sunshine in your smile. Hanakotoba interprets a yellow tulip as: one-sided love. To further complicate things, there are hundreds of floral dictionaries, each one slightly different.

The meanings have also changed through the years. For instance, daffodils were considered a symbol of chivalry during Victorian times, whereas today daffodils are a symbol of hope.

Some floral interpretations, however, stretch across all cultures and have become fully ingrained in our perceptions, such as:

- Red roses meaning true love. It is still the most popular flower to convey the sentiment on Valentine's Day.

- Poppies worn for Remembrance Day.

- Extending an olive branch meaning a desire to make peace.

- Finding a four-leaf clover meaning good luck.

- Mistletoe meaning kiss me.

- A white lily meaning purity, still popular as an Easter Lily.

Designing to speak to emotions is a subtle and sensitive skill that delivers truly great work and transcends aesthetics.

A well-designed arrangement is a physical object that becomes personal, a way for us to connect with and respond to each other. For instance: sympathy flowers can celebrate a life, love, and memories shared, and the design can show concern for those we care for.

The secret to cultivating this skill is to focus on the emotions you, as a designer, invest in the design, and the emotions you experience when looking at your own designs. Your customers come to you because they love what you do and trust you to relay an important message. That means there is already a connection between you. If you feel it, they will feel it.

Our busy schedules often prevent us from acknowledging our emotions while designing. But when we create, we instinctively draw on some emotion that dictates every design decision. The real challenge is to intentionally direct this instinct and consistently create appropriate and meaningful work. This involves taking time to deliberately think about, and note down, your design choices and the reasons for making them. The following questions can guide you through this process. There is no right or wrong answer. There is only your answer.

🌾 Elements and principles of design: Consider lines, patterns, space, texture, and colour. How will each affect an emotional reaction to a design? How will scale, contrast, or balance and the other principles of design affect the way you interpret the design?

🌾 Accessories: What are your accessory preferences, and why? What is the emotion behind choosing one type of ribbon over the other? How can you stretch accessories to encompass other emotions? What does a happy bow look like? How can it be adapted to say, "I am thinking of you in this sad time"?

🌾 Imagery: What images or symbols do you associate with different emotions? In sympathy work, designers are often asked to craft wreaths, pillows, hearts, religious signs, symbols, and emblems. How do you incorporate these in your designs and remain authentic in your own creative style?

🌾 Cultural beliefs: How are your design choices affected by your, your customer's, or the show's culture? A design, for instance, entered into a botanical show would require more unusual flowers. Are there certain cultures or communities for which your designs are more, or less, appropriate?

🌾 Consideration: What steps do you take to consider the well-being and emotions of people who will steward, place, take care of the delivery of, maintain, and dismantle your design? How will your design avoid frustration? Are there third parties, such as a funeral director, household or hospital staff, church official, gallery curator, etc., to liaise with?

🌾 Logistics: How would transport, location, travel, and delivery times affect your decisions?

You will be ready, even during busy times, to create designs with meaning, by continually investing the time to broaden your signature style to include a wide range of emotions.

reciprocity
the fine art of sharing creativity

"*you don't find your effortless style in things you think you should create. you find your effortless style in the things you just create.***"**

Over the years, the *My Creative Workbook* website has grown steadily and organically by word of mouth with a few more "looks" and "signups" every day. I never set out to create what it has become. *My Creative Workbook* started out as just that, an online workbook to capture my creative research and an all-in-one-place recipe book for me to access over time.

Today it is a creative resource used by floral artists, designers, and crafters from all over the world.

I have come to understand that what I have accomplished on *My Creative Workbook* captures what really matters to me. In doing so, I have learned about my own creative currencies. What I work for. Over the years I have also learned how we, as a creative community, define the process of giving and taking fairly—reciprocity. In this chapter, we will consider how we can share our own original work, and that of other craftsmen, in an ethical, fair, supportive, and encouraging way.

What matters to me?

Making my art. I want to, one day, make a design as powerful as a good piece of music. And when I do that, I will share it with you.

And, while working on that goal, I get to see the creativity that sharing my work inspires. How talented and creative people give an idea, that I thought of and shared, a twist all of their own. With this in mind, I have tweaked the format of my website after its first year. I have since then dedicated time and energy on creating a library of over a thousand of my designs and tutorials aimed at providing inspiration and value to this community that has assembled around my website. This is the driving force behind my website. As you continue reading, you will see this repeated, over and over, in my opinions.

Usually when we look at compensation for work, the first currency that springs to mind is money.

Yes, money is a currency. I have an asking price for this book. And you pay me money if you want to own a copy. This is a clear transaction. But money is not the only currency. My website is a good example of this. When I started *My Creative Workbook*, no one was a blogger for money. I am rather glad about that because it gave me a broader understanding of currencies. I do not charge money for my weekly design training. But if you value my work and get some benefit out of my weekly training, you will want to encourage me to continue my work and my website. How? Well, this is where it gets fascinating. Over time, you, the readers have figured out what I value, my currency. Some of you tell me that you value my work when we meet, some of you come and look at my new design every week, some send me encouraging emails, show me your work inspired by my work, some connect with me on social media, some click on my "send Christine a smile" button above my design, and some of you share my work with other people who might enjoy it. And those people visit my site.

And because connecting with like-minded, creative people is valuable to me, I create more work to share the following week. Give and take. It is no less of a transaction as exchanging money is.

Furthermore, because I am not dependent on blog views or held hostage by algorithms to sustain my site, I have the freedom to choose and set my own goals.

Merely driving traffic to my site has never been my goal. But sharing my work with creative and committed readers is.

I wanted to craft well-researched design how-tos of techniques that come in handy after you have done your basic flower-arranging training, and I wanted to make these techniques freely available to anyone, regardless of work experience, skill level, location, club affiliation, or access to advanced training. I also wanted to craft art from readily available objects (such as twigs, cardboard, and autumn leaves) with just a few flowers that make crafting with nature, and continuous learning, affordable. It was what I looked for when I started out, but did not find. So I created it.

This is my place where I get to share my experimental work away from my usual constraints.

I can make just about whatever I like. I do not need to insist you look at my work. And you get to choose whether you look, or not.

Which really is just our play-nice rules.

Do you remember the play-nice rules you learned as a child? It went something like this:

🌿 We are gentle when we play.

🌿 We share, take turns, and ask lonely children if they would like to join in our games.

🌿 We respect everyone's games and let other children get on with their games.

🌿 We look after the playground.

🌿 We tell the teacher on duty if there is a problem.

Not much has changed, really. I am sure you can easily see how this is applicable to the interactions in our creative community.

Let's look at sharing.

It is worth mentioning that all creative works are copyright protected by default. Unfortunately, a watermark will not protect your work (nor images of your work) from being taken and used by someone else. Only nonnegotiable, ethical sharing does that. So what is ethical sharing?

ethical sharing, as a rule of thumb, includes these ideas:

- If you took the picture of your original work, you can share it as you wish.

- If the picture was not taken by you or if the piece was not made by you, share it and credit it. No exceptions.

- If you do not know who made it, ask the person who shared it to credit it so that you can share and credit it. This way we break the chain of unethical sharing.

- Crediting social media or a website as a source is not enough. This is not an idea of, or a design made by, or a picture taken by a website. Credit the artist, the person who did the work. Where possible, link back to them and reward them for great work shared in whatever currency you have, in this case exposure.

- Letting someone know that you are sharing their work is always appreciated.

- Never add to or edit someone else's pictures without explicit permission. Adding your signature or removing the watermark on someone else's design is never okay. Never. Okay.

- If you are profiting from an image, you, at the very least, need permission from the owner and, at best, you should share the profit. Do not use another designer's images in your promotions, craft works, or training.

- Remember there is a person behind the web pages creating the art and sharing creativity with you. That is a great gift. Respect that. Respect them.

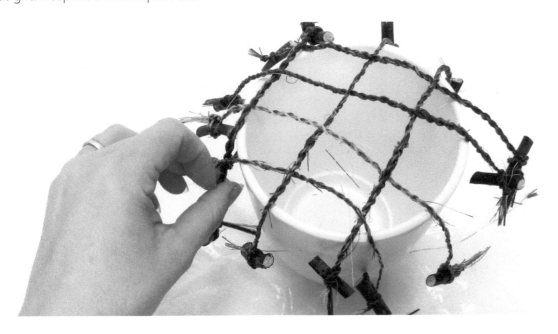

As a supportive and encouraging creative community, we like to take things a step further than just doing the right thing.

Here are a few suggestions on how we can support and encourage other floral craftsmen in our creative community:

🌿 Support an artist financially. Buy their stuff. Sign up for their workshops and demonstrations. Give their classes as a gift to someone else who is creative. Donate to their projects, buy their books, and commission them to create designs with your products or for your events. Be fair.

🌿 Introduce your creative inspiration to your other creative inspirations. Share people who are doing great work. Help to promote them and their art.

🌿 I have a "send Christine a smile" button on my website, and I can tell you that I appreciate every single "smile" I get. It shows me that you are out there and you are walking the creative journey with me. I also have a pin board in my design room and that is where your emails, cards, and notes go. These notes mean so much to me. It makes me feel supported and valued.

🌿 Yes, a social media like is great, and so is a re-tweet or a share. Be generous with those. But those alone can be a bit disheartening, especially if the artist took great effort to create what was shared. If you feel comfortable doing so, show the artist that you are not only noticing her creative effort but you took time to appreciate it. Stay a while and type a comment. Write the email. Likes are appreciated, but a kind comment can inspire on a low-inspiration day

🌿 Support others in the currency they value, whether it is money, likes, compliments, recognition, or a sincere thank you. Whatever call to action there is, take it. With that being said: be mindful of how much of your creative energy goes into convincing people to click like buttons, and how much time you spend clicking like buttons. If this kind of interaction is a strong currency for you and if it adds to your creative process, great. But make sure you work for the currency you truly value and don't get distracted by what seems to be of value to others but doesn't feed you.

🌿 Thank you. Sometimes that is all it takes. If an artist shared a skill with you, opened a door for you when he really did not have to, supported you, or went out of her way to reply to your email, write the thank you reply. It strengthens the connection and creates a support network shared by all creatives creating. Thank You.

While exploring ways of sharing work, it is impossible not to venture into some gray areas such as inspiring and being inspired by work we see online.

At some point, you will come across something, somewhere, that you are convinced you thought of first. I am often asked, "Aren't you scared someone will steal what you are doing?" Truth is, it is never easy sending my idea out in the world all on its own.

It helps to remember that your creative idea did not spring from your personal, wholly isolated, well of greatness. While you are working on your next greatest idea, there is someone (more likely a few someones) working on, or thinking about, the exact same thing. That is why trends catch on everywhere at once. Even so, it is hard for any designer to see his ideas used by others.

We belong to an ecosystem of creativity. We are all inspired by what we see. Creativity flows like a current all around the world. Our creativity feeds on everything that our senses are exposed to. In the words of Aristotle: "It is not once, nor twice, but times without number, that the same idea makes an appearance around the world." The process of creativity is a group effort performed by creative individuals. Even individuals who seem to be, or think they are, isolated.

So, the first part of my advice would be to give the designer the benefit of doubt. It really is quite possible that both you, and another designer, thought of doing something very similar, but not quite identical. No two designs can ever truly be exactly the same. There are just too many variables. Take comfort in the fact that your style will show through. Your choice of material will add a distinctive twist. Those little touches that you so effortlessly add will set your work apart.

And my second piece of advice would be to change your perspective. Let's say someone saw your idea, loved it, and copied it. Now think about this: You have made someone stop scrolling. He noticed your work, in a world where we are so overwhelmed with stunning design ideas and colourful pictures that very little really sticks, much less motivates us to create.

That person took the time to really understand your work, enough time to make another piece just like it. Maybe you already had the raw material in your design room or growing in your garden or you picked it up along the way on your morning walk, while the person you inspired did not. He loved your work enough to take the time to actually go search for it.

You have to admit, that kind of influence is extraordinary.

And YOU did that. And because you did it, you can do it again. A copy of a work will never have quite the same magic as the original because it did not originate from the place where extraordinary comes from. Your idea can be copied, yes; but your creativity cannot. You move right on and go make your next stop-scrolling-and-really-notice creation. This is what masters do. They inspire and teach … and continue creating and growing. You are a thought leader, a true influencer, and an inspiration. Go make more stuff.

And if you still feel offended because you did not get credit? Well, when we look at a collection of copied designs, we can clearly see the inconsistency in style, effort, and heart. You don't even have to tell us, because we already know. All you need to do is create another … and another … and another. Your body of work, your acts of creation, will make your unmistakable and effortless style instantly recognizable.

Let the imitations pale in comparison.

A creative idea is not less valuable if anyone can actually physically make this. The real value of a creative idea is found in the bit that no one else thought of making this like you did.

Now let's look at the flip side. Once you reach a certain skill level, being influenced by and being overly inspired by other designers is, in my experience, more damaging than constructive.

I basically subscribe to the idea that we have a creative voice inside us that comes up with these ideas. It is your interpreter. It takes all the ideas you are exposed to, distills them into something uniquely "you," and whispers it back to you. The more you listen to that voice, the clearer the instructions. The reverse is also true. Every time you use someone else's idea, it becomes harder for you to hear your own creativity and come up with your own ideas. It damages your ability to be original. You hurt your creative voice's feelings, and it goes and sits in a corner and gives you the silent treatment. Copying a master's work is a great starting point to learn and develop your basic skills. Every technique you master becomes another mark in the measuring stick of what is good art to you. But copying is only an entry point. It is your responsibility to move beyond imitation.

- Be inspired by techniques and not designs or styles. This is what I focus on providing on *My Creative Workbook*. Sharing how I made it adds value to what I made. When I say: I made a basket design, I mean I made a basket, here is the design. And I share it as inspiration. We may take inspiration, which means we may open ourselves to allow other designers' work to inspire us, and let it change us, but these inspirational things are not ours for keeps. They are ours to enjoy and then interpret through our own work.

- Be selective in your influences and know when to decline input. If someone's advice is just not where you are heading creatively or is intimidating, or their work is so amazing that it paralyzes you and keeps you from developing, you have every right to say: "Thank you, but no thank you."

- Incorporating giving credit, attribution, and compliments as a personal design policy is a great way to combat dulling your own voice. It keeps your work honest. You have not invested enough of yourself in the work if your design is so close to the original source of inspiration that it would be embarrassing to your creative soul to give credit.

- Search out people who are in line with your design journey but are strong in areas where you are not, and ask for help. This does not need to be a face-to-face workshop, although it sometimes helps to see an expert in action. It can be on-the-job training, a flower club, an apprenticeship, a book, or video tutorial, or even a website with inspirational images. Join or create communities where you feel supported and valued.

... and anyway, we would all like to see where you can take the craft. Please show us your way of crafting with nature. Listen to your creative voice and figure stuff out. Interpret the information and inspiration you are exposed to. Show us what only you can possibly make. Something far better than even you thought possible. Your contribution to our craft. And pass it along.

do more than you have to

"if your technique is not quite right, practice and fix it next time. if you are working without passion, fix that right now."

Sometimes we fail when we try to create something for which there is no how-to.

Granted, sometimes we succeed and create something so spectacular that it rocks your flower world.

In this chapter, I look at the sometimes ... when we fail.

Sometimes we get stuff wrong. We read the competition schedule wrong. Your perfectly planned and executed design just looks wrong. You submit your work to a publication and get rejected because you misjudged what they were looking for.

You and me both. You and me and every other person out there making stuff that matters.

It is so tempting to believe that if we show up, do the work, and make an effort we WILL succeed. I believe that is only the beginning of the story. If we show up, do the work, and make an effort, we get a shot at success. No work, no shot.

Sure, if you do not put your work out there, out there has way less opportunity to reject you. But you also have nothing out there to give you a shot at a "yes."

And if things go wrong?

Make your art anyway.

Now, I have enough experience to tell you success and failure are relative. There are times when success leads you down a road that you did not want to be on and failure leads you to greater understanding.

Make your art anyway.

I can also tell you that only you can really define what meaningful success or paralyzing failure is.

Make your art anyway.

This is even more true for really, really big setbacks and near apocalyptic failures (I am an artist and do not lack in the sense of drama department).

It takes strength to continue making your art when you have been knocked down. It takes courage to make art that heals. And when you feel that you lack both strength and courage, in my experience, a healthy helping of stubbornness can give you a push to see what you can create with what you have left. Ironically, you might even find that it is in these times that it is easiest for you to access your unique and effortless style.

It is when things get really ugly that we most need to create pretty things.

I speak a lot about your creative spark, that inner voice that you need to develop and protect with respectful work. It is a powerful resource to draw upon when you create your art. It is also a resource to draw upon while you create you.

It is in those moments when I am designing better than I have imagined, that I am aware of that creative bit in me. Things are okay because I am exactly who I need to be to create this. But more so, if I do not create this it will be lost because no one else can. In those moments that I challenge myself just enough, things somehow happen and the art flows effortlessly. I completely lose track of time. I feel grounded and rooted and connected with what is important to me. It gives me something to hang onto when I am doing the stuff that happens between those moments. It gives me a resource to draw upon so that I don't get swept away in moments of feeling overwhelmed.

We experience trauma in a similar way to plants. When something happens and we feel severed from the vital things that usually give us roots, we also need some kind and compassionate, and "me-specific" conditioning.

So create, make pretty stuff, and keep your creative flow open. Be kind to yourself. Provide yourself with the best possible environmental conditions for you to continue making your art. Because, you see, success is knowing in your gut that you just created something rather exceptional. This is it. Success is knowing you gave this your all—win or lose, sell or stay, published or rejected. What you have created to put out there is not one single petal less than your best.

Next time you pick up your tools ... well, it starts again, doesn't it? But not quite from the beginning. You now have a new standard to strive to. You measure your success from your starting point to where you are now. Your next successful design will be a bit better than the one before. Value your process, not just the end results. You are stacking your odds at getting your shot.

Every time you do just a little bit more than you have to...

added extras and finishing touches

natural stain

Using fruit, berries, flowers, and grasses to naturally stain design details for floral art relies on the same techniques as using water-based paint or dye. All the colours can be mixed to create the exact colour you want.

You can either boil the plant material to create a dye bath or crush or grate it to make a dye rub.

For stronger colours, allow the items to soak longer in the dye bath. Because we are mostly staining decorative objects, simply rubbing the stain on, for the most part, does the job.

For a more permanent stain, mix a fixative of 1/2 cup salt to every 8 cups of water for the berries, and 1/4 cup vinegar for every cup of water for the plant material.

Soak the fiber, wood, or object you want to stain in the fixative for about an hour before rinsing in cool water and then staining it.

Soak both sides of wooden shapes at once so that the piece doesn't warp.

how-to | # stain sisal with berries

Juice the berries in a blender.

Soak the dry sisal fibers in the purple berry juice.

Rinse the soaked fibers.

Set aside to dry.

Untangle the fibers and add to the design.

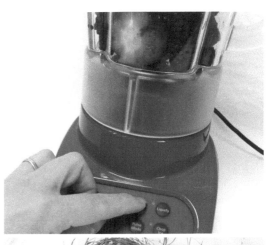

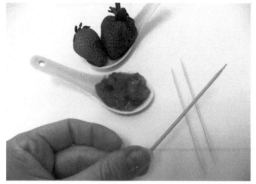

strawberry pink

Crush the ripe strawberries and soak the skewers. Set aside to dry.

raspberry red

For a darker red stain, use raspberries.

blue

For a blue stain, use blueberries, pansies, or violets.

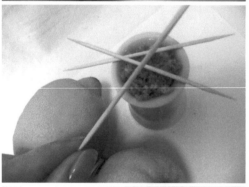

brightest yellow

Zest a lemon or an orange to rub the skewer with. It also smells great!

grass green

The water left over from cooked spinach works really well as a natural green dye, but you can also use grass (for a more yellowish green) or green herbs such as parsley (for an emerald green) or mint (for a camouflage green).

mud brown

Use leftover coffee grounds to rub or soak the skewers in. The longer you steep the skewer, the darker the colour.

spicy shades of yellow, red and orange

Mix spices into a paste as a dye-rub. Try paprika and red pepper for a vibrant red, and curry powder or turmeric for a yellow to orange stain.

orange

For an orange stain, use grated carrot.

yellow

Onion skins stain to a brownish yellow.

earthy orange red

I use rooibos tea for a natural reddish tint. If I am staining a large surface, I use the entire teabag as a brush. For a more vibrant red, you can use beetroot, rose hips, or red onions.

stain a paperback pumpkin with rooibos tea

Brew a strong batch of tea in a shallow dish. I used South African rooibos tea to get an earthy, orange-red stain.

Dip the edge of the cut book in the tea. Fold the pages back to soak the book a few pages at a time.

Roll the book in the tea, soaking just the edges.

Squeeze out most of the tea.

Flip through the wet pages to separate them and to add a bit of a curve.

Set the book pumpkin aside to dry completely.

Paint lines with a paintbrush to stain your pumpkin a more vibrant orange.

how-to | cut a paperback pumpkin

I love reading. In fact, part of my definition of true happiness is having a half-read book with me. And I treasure my books. Which means, cutting up a book is rather painful ... but not more painful than a book with an unhappy ending. So, here is a craft to turn books with unhappy endings into something beautiful to look at.

Rip the front and back cover from the paperback books and break the spine of the book by bending the pages back, about 15 pages at a time, to fan the book open.

Place the book upright. You will notice the book flares open on the pages where the spine is broken. If it is not flared enough, go back and do less pages at a time.

I used five books for my pumpkin.

Use a saucer to trace a circle onto the book. Let the saucer overlap the book end slightly to give the shape a flat base. Curve the top to be slightly flatter.

With a very sharp knife, cut out the shape and cut through the glued spine.

Glue the books together and allow the pages to flair open naturally.

The spines of the books create a cavity perfect for a water source for your flowers.

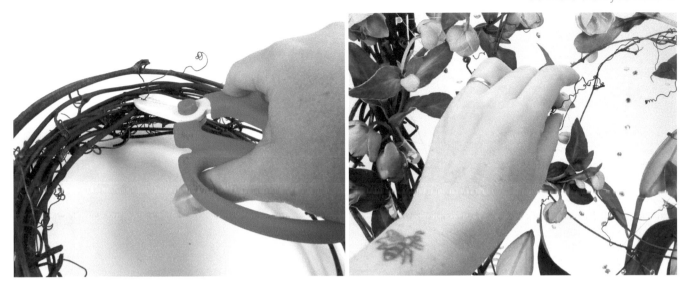

how-to | # glue in tendrils

I cut tendrils from vine wreaths to add as design details. It adds contrast to delicate designs without distracting.

Make sure to add the tendrils in such a way that they add to the vibrancy of the design. The tendrils should always point in a general up direction and never curve in a way that makes them appear wilted.

how-to | # place a dewdrop crystal using a pin

Pick the crystal up with a pin.

Simply press the pin under the crystal so that the glue part sticks to the pin, making it easy to lift away from the packaging.

Carefully place it in the design without bruising even the most delicate petals, adhering the tiny crystals exactly where you want them.

how-to | # prevent browning with lemon

The ascorbic acid in lemon keeps plant material from turning brown because the oxygen reacts to the acid before it will react with the polyphenol oxidase in the plant material.

Spritz a bit of lemon on cut fruit before adding it into a design.

If you need to cut away a petal, you can also paint the wound with a few drops of lemon to prevent visible brown lines.

Flowers like gardenias are really sensitive and will start to brown as soon as they are exposed to air and will bruise because they react to the oils on your fingers. Spray the flowers with a weak solution of water (about 90%) and lemon (about 10%) just before designing with them. Touch your fingers to the lemon juice and keep your hands wet as you design. Preferably, touch only the stems. If you must touch the flower, touch it at the back.

Prevent browning when you detail foliage by dipping your scissors in lemon juice.

how-to | # add a stem to crystals

If you need the beads to softly float above your design, it is better to thread or glue them onto a twig or stem. If you glue the beads to some of the flowers, they would disappear in the mass of twigs and flowers.

Glue the beads to the ends of sticks. Now the beads can be inserted just like the flower stems and tied with the rest of the design to hover like two shiny snowflakes.

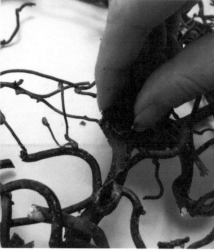

| # encourage moss and lichen to grow on a design

Moss and lichen feed on dust and ambient moisture. It is actually a good sign to see them appear—it means you do not live in an area with high air pollution. The lower the air quality, the less likely the growth of moss and lichen.

Remove a clump of moss and clean as much soil as possible without breaking up the clump or damaging the spores.

Dip a clump of moss in yogurt. Make sure you saturate the clump. The ratio of moss to yogurt is not really important.

You can also add honey to the yogurt, or mix beer and sugar, or use buttermilk. I find the yogurt-moss mixture works fine all on its own.

Paint the object (here a twig wreath and cement bowl) with yogurt, using the moss as a brush. This will transfer the spores onto the twigs.

Dab and wiggle the moss as you go along.

Any porous, rough surface that retains water will grow moss. It takes a while. If all goes well, I will see the moss appearing on my wreath within 10 days, but it can take up to a month to have real growth.

Choose the right location for your moss garden. It needs natural light but a shady, damp position is best. Emulate nature.

Your moss garden needs to be cool and wet. Lichen and moss become dormant when they become too hot and dry.

Protect the moss-yogurt mixture from rain so that it doesn't wash away. Mist the area regularly and cover with a plastic bag if necessary.

how-to | # string beads on a blade of grass

Cut the blade of grass at a sharp angle and thread the grass into the bead.

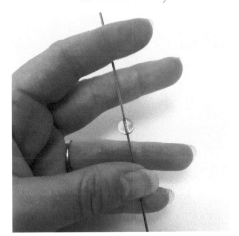

how-to | # pour water without disturbing design elements

Pour water over the back of a spoon. This creates a gentler stream of water that can be controlled.

You can also pour water over the back of your cupped hand and let the gentle stream spill into the design.

This is also great for topping up water in an intricate design.

how-to | # sugar-frost flowers, fruit, and foliage

Paint or dip edible flowers (such as pansies) in egg white.

Sprinkle with sugar and set aside so that the egg white dries.

| # make a tassel

Rip a handful of flax with a pin or a Kenzan.

Tie the flax in the middle.

Fold the flax in half and wrap a strand of flax around the bundle. Tie with a double knot.

how-to | buff a pom-pom

Rip a bundle of flax. Buff the bundle by running your knife over the flax to remove most of the green pulp.

Cut two circles out of cardboard. Cut a hole in each circle.

Run a strand of the flax between the two cardboard layers. This will be used to tie the pom-pom, so take care not to wrap it.

Wrap the buffed white strands of flax around the cardboard.

Wiggle the strand that is sandwiched between the cardboard, along the inside of the cardboard, so that it lies all the way around. If it gets lost along the way, you can always add another strand in the end.

When the cardboard is wrapped, cut the strands along the outer edge of the circles.

Pull the strand, or if it got lost, split the cardboard open and wrap a strand around the entire bundle of flax.

Tie with a double knot, remove the cardboard, and fluff out the pom-pom.

critters

how-to | ## zigzag a dragonfly

The body of the dragonfly is made up of the traditional zigzag pattern of a Palm Sunday craft technique to make a lantern.

Split a leaf or blade of grass in three, right along the hard vein. You will need two blades for each dragonfly.

Place the two blades together and start the zigzag folding pattern.

Sandwich the blades of grass with the harder vein facing in. You will be folding the blades around these.

Fold the first blade of grass over its partner, then fold the opposite blade over its partner.

Slip the opposite blades through the fold to create a zigzag pattern and pull the blades all the way through to secure.

To start the weaving pattern, fold the first leaf over. Fold the next blade over the first. Fold the next blade over this blade. Fold the last blade over the first and slip it through the fold to secure. Pull the blades of grass to tighten the fold. This is the basic folding pattern. Repeat this to make the lantern/dragonfly body.

Continue to fold the blades over. Build up the pattern for the dragonfly body.

With the body part done, split the blade open, letting the softer blades flop over and the two harder veins extend.

Fold the blades, two to each side, and tie a bow. The loops form the wings, and the bow-ends, the legs.

Knot the veins to create the upper body, and knot again for the large head. Cut any dangling pieces short.

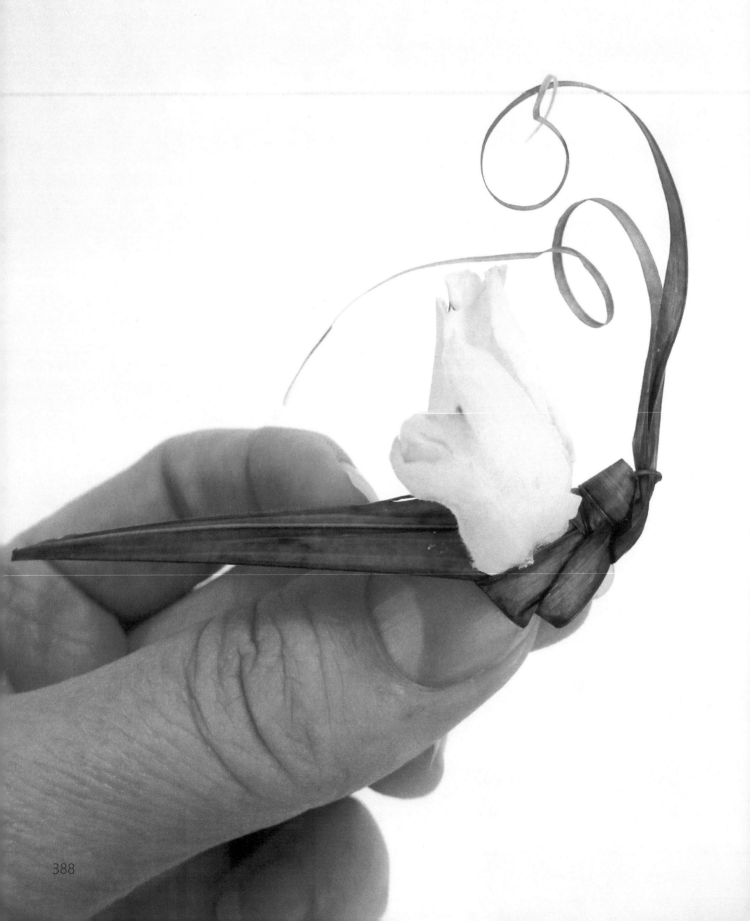

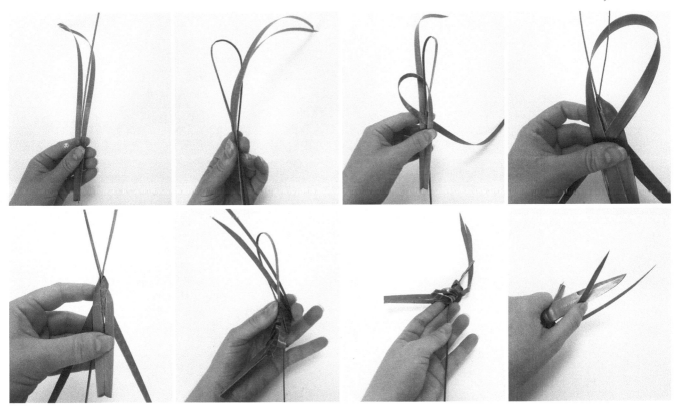

how-to | fold hopper-flies (grasshoppers and butterflies)

Split the leaf in three using a pin, separating the hard center vein from the leaf at both sides. Leave the last 2 cm (3/4 in) intact at the side that was connected to the palm.

Carefully run your nail along the vein to soften it so that it's more pliable. Fold the vein back on itself and tuck under the leaf where it's still connected. It might be easier for you to use a tiny bit of putty or floral fix to keep the vein in place while you practice doing this. Later, you will find it's easy to hold in place while you weave the body.

Fold one side under and then over the vein. Pull tight. Do the same with the other side and pull tight.

Continue weaving the body two or three more times, depending on the length of your blade of grass or palm leaf.

Create feelers (antennae) by tucking the two sides of the leaf into the vein loop and pulling the vein snug. Separate the side strips and carefully run your nail through the length of each to curl as you would ribbon.

Finish off the body by weaving the long center vein around itself and cut short. Cut the tail end if required.

You can now add leaves for wings or cut the leftover vein in two, for legs to tuck into the body.

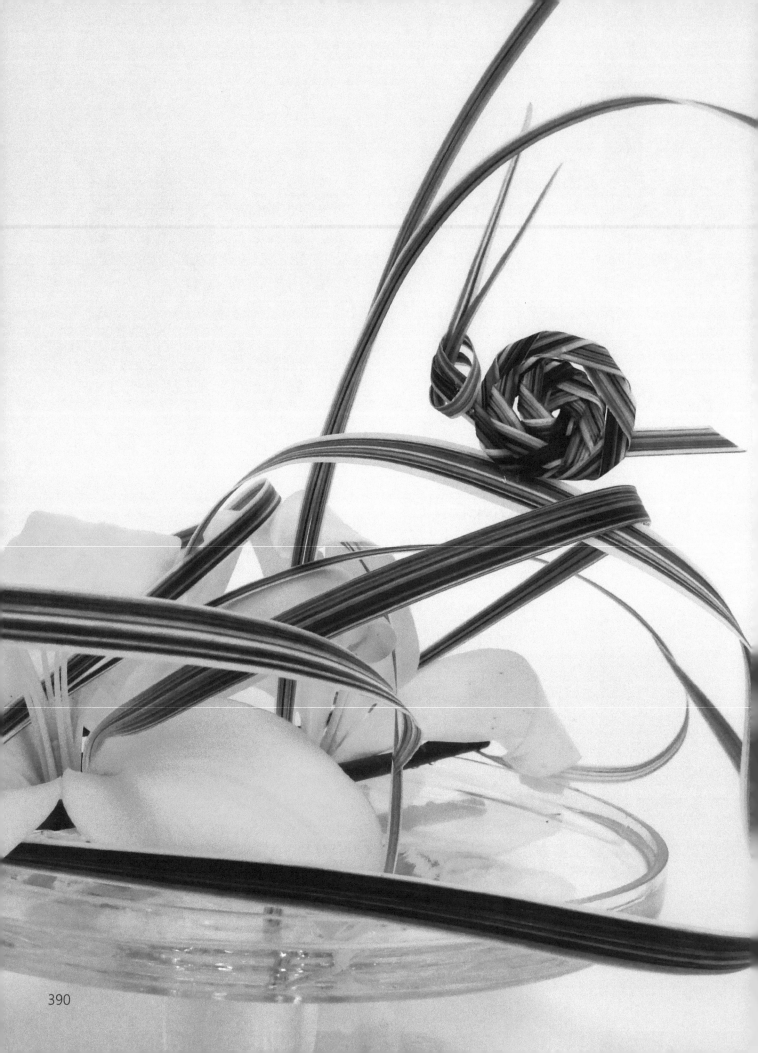

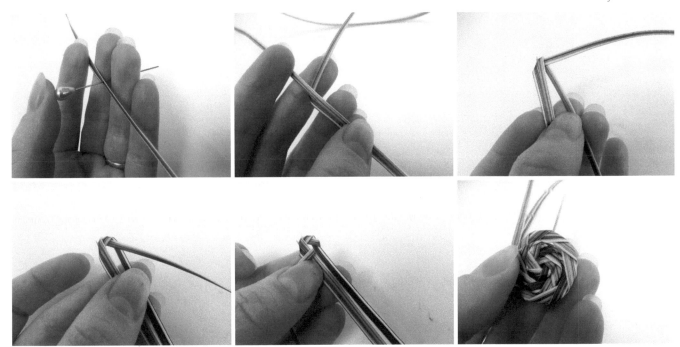

how-to | spiral a grass snail

The shell of the snail is made with a traditional spiral rose craft technique.

Split a long blade of grass with a pin.

Split from where the leaf becomes soft enough to fold up to the tip, leaving the harder stem side intact.

Fold the left side of the split blade at an angle and behind the other half.

Fold the right side under the first half. This is your basic spiral folding pattern. Continue to fold the grass to create a snail shell spiral.

Simply fold the next blade under the first, at an angle ... and the next one under the one before.

The folded grass will start to spiral out.

Weave the harder stem part through the spiral to the back, and the soft split ends to the front.

Knot the split ends to create the snail head.

Cut the body end shorter and secure with glue if necessary.

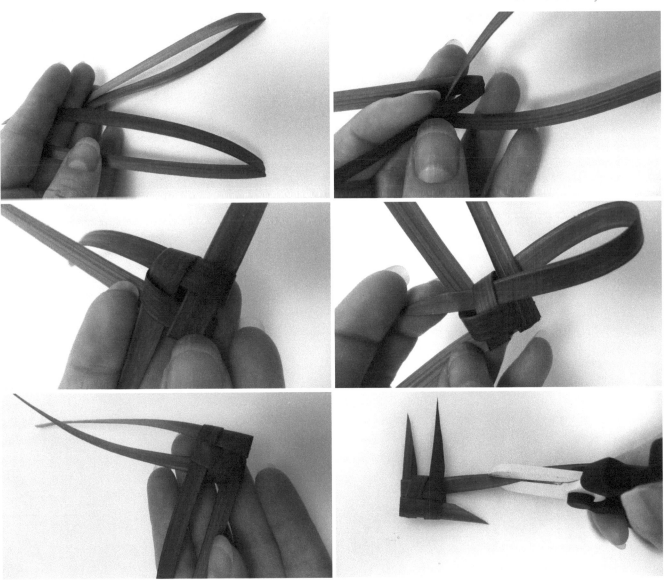

how-to | fold a foliage fish

Fold two blades of grass in half. Slip the first blade into the second blade and pull the two blades tight.

Start to weave the grass. Hold the grass so that the folded ends point down and the dangling grass faces up.

Fold the top blade facing up over to weave through the ends pointing to the side.

Fold the back blade that is facing to the side over and through the loop you created with the first fold.

Fold the dangling blade of grass that faces up through the loop you just created. Weave the last blade through the remaining loop and pull tight.

Flip the fish over and repeat on the other side. Pull the ends tight.

Cut the fins and the tail short, if you prefer.

394

about me

"luxury is working until you can say: this is the best I can do."

My accent is from South Africa, but I am a Canadian living in Vancouver, beautiful British Columbia, with my husband, Marius.

I work as a floral design skills developer and mostly write and talk about floral craftsmanship. I am a floral design partner and columnist for the popular wedding magazine *DIY Weddings* and take part in design shows, competitions, and demonstrations.

I am inspired by good old-fashioned craftsmanship. I often use ancient, cultural, and traditional techniques but in a thoroughly contemporary way. My floral art is the result of trying to bring these two ends - the old and the new - together.

My work takes time. It is detail oriented and deliberate, which is probably why I enjoy designing for publications and competitions. After spending days building a single delicate armature, it will naturally fade - but the photograph of the work lives on.

Like any craftsman, I dedicate my time to developing my craft and, in turn, I teach. Wednesdays have become my favourite day of the week because I connect with all my flower friends when I post a new design, with its related step-by-step tutorials, on my website.

I am passionate about floral craftsmanship and continuous development.

If you have learned a skill, teach someone else how to do it.

If you meet a designer who has perfected a skill, learn from her.

This keeps our design skills alive and cross-pollinates expertise between craft and art forms, creating a stronger skill set that ensures floral art stays relevant and continues to thrive.

We can buy flowers anywhere. A skilled floral artist translates flowers into a story of emotion.

It is our skills that set us apart.

Crafting something purely for the sake of creating beauty has been a lifeline for me. My work matters to me. Greatly. And I thank you, from that creative bit inside me, if it has somehow come to matter to you.

Every good wish,

Christine

Master Floral Artist

Acknowledgement:

In the chapter about reciprocity I mentioned that I truly don't believe we create alone. Writing The Effortless Floral Craftsman was such a beautiful and humbling affirmation of that.

I wrote this book sitting alone (and wifi-less!) in a coffee shop trying to figure out my creative processes for myself. I agonized over every word for years!

But it turns out, even then, I wasn't truly alone. Today, almost a year after I wrote the last words for The Effortless Floral Craftsman, I am still discovering words written by artists and thought leaders that are reassuringly similar to my thoughts expressed in these pages.

As an experimental artist who mostly work alone it is comforting to remember that we are all together on this endless journey to master our craft.

Creativity is a collaboration, even if you are not aware of it at the time.

Further Reading:

Seth Godin: The Dip ('quit or be exceptional, average is for losers')

Malcolm Gladwell

Game theory

Flow theory

Sir Ken Robinson (education)

Floral Art Clubs, especially W.A.F.A (rules)

Paul Felix, Sian Ellis, Tom Quinn: The book of forgotten crafts (the need to keep our craft skills alive)

Hideyuki Oka: How to wrap 5 more eggs (tradition)

Wikipedia (for the information on Latin plant names)

George Lucas: Star Wars ('there can be no master without an apprentice')

Biomimicry (to innovate as nature does)

Tara Brach (how we respond to trauma)

Leonardo Da Vinci

Aristotle

Terry Pratchett

Creative Commons (copyright law)

... and thank you also to all the creative and talented writers, designers and flower buddies who inspire me in real life and through the My Creative Workbook website every day.

For additional views of the designs featured in this book and more detailed how-tos, register as an Effortless Floral Craftsman on:
www.christinedebeer.ca
You need a copy of the book to complete the sign-up.
You can also use the #EffortlessFloralCraftsman hashtag when talking about the book on social media
(@chris10debeer) so that we can connect.

397

flower guide

Phormium (New Zealand Flax) 1, 22, 23, 29, 46, 47, 48, 49, 50, 51, 52, 53, 54, 55, 56, 57, 62, 63, 95, 165, 204, 205, 227, 228, 229, 230, 231, 238, 239, 240, 241, 248, 249, 250, 251, 252, 253, 310, 311, 327, 352, 353, 362, 363, 384, 385, 386, 387, 392, 393

Physalis (Chinese lantern) 4, 111, 116, 117, 118, 368, 402, 403

Prosthechea Cochleata Orchid (Octopus) 208

Prunus (Cherry) 284

R

Ranunculus (Buttercup) 320, 354, 355

Rosa Canina (Rosehip) 30, 206, 304, 305, 370, 371

Rosa (Rose) 32, 34, 68, 71, 98, 99, 166, 167, 168, 186, 188, 189, 200, 201, 202, 203, 274, 275, 388, 400, 401

Rubus Idaeus (Raspberry) 374

S

Salix matsudana 'Tortuosa' (Curly Willow) 18, 25, 65, 74, 75, 76, 78, 79, 81, 101, 140, 141, 180, 181, 191, 214, 215, 217, 242, 243, 244, 245, 254, 255, 274, 280, 281, 282, 283, 285, 304, 305, 322, 323, 328, 329, 336, 337, 358,, 359, 360, 361, 362, 363, 366, 367, 373, 378, 379

Senecio Radicans (String of Beans) 70, 212

Senecio Rowleyanus (String of Pearls) 30, 84, 312

Solanum Integrifolium (Pumpkin Tree Plant) 304, 305

Spinacia Oleracea (Spinach) 371, 374

Strelitzia Reginae (Bird of Paradise) 300

Succulents (Assorted rosette shaped eg: Echeveria 104, 105, 312

Tillandsia (Assorted air plants) 106, 107, 108, 109, 150, 152, 208, 312, 330, 331

Tillandsia Usneoides (Spanish moss) 9, 109, 174, 176, 177, 266, 267, 269, 317, 330, 331

Tulipa (Tulip) 92, 100, 157, 295, 296, 297, 298, 299

V

Viola (pansy) 123, 150, 152, 180, 196, 197, 322, 323, 372, 383

Vitis Vinifera (Grape Vine) 4, 19, 32, 34, 76, 78, 79, 134, 136, 137, 139, 144, 145, 156, 174, 176, 177, 266, 267, 269, 286, 287, 317, 330, 331, 378, 379, 402, 403

Z

Zantedeschia (Arum lily) 160, 163, 196, 299, 352, 353

what is in a name?

Designers often share that they get stuck on figuring out what is the "right" name for the plant material they are using, and how to pronounce it. And with good reason! Especially if you are traveling across borders to design.

Of course we need a working knowledge of plant types and names. Apart from avoiding confusion, knowing the botanical names also provides us with clues as to how we need to condition the plants and which techniques would be more suitable when we design. But the quest for the "right" name should not be so intimidating a task that it becomes a stumbling block in our creative work.

Nomenclature is the method of assigning unique names to plant material. Botanical nomenclature is the naming of plants from a scientific point of view. These botanical names are governed by the International Code of Botanical Nomenclature.

Now, here's where things get confusing. We don't always speak botanical nomenclature. We often speak in the vernacular.

As an example, let's explore the Rosaceae family: If Snow White's stepmother offered her a *malus*, I suspect the fairy tale would have been much shorter. (The Latin word malus means "bad" or "wicked" but it is, of course, the scientific name for *apple* -a word which sounds perfectly wholesome.)

To add to the confusion let's consider that the apple tree is, in fact, part of the rose family (*Rosaceae*). It would again be a completely different story if Snow White was offered *a rose*. Furthermore any self respecting rose lover would by now be wondering *but what type of rose...*

There is not just one system that roses are classified in. If you get around all the variations and opinions, growers, breeders, and rose lovers will (maybe) agree that roses are placed in three main groups: Wild roses, Old Garden roses, and Modern Garden roses (and any rose classified after 1867 is considered modern). At this point, they will already be arguing about "rose hybrids" and "flower form" and "growth habits."

There are at least 100 species and thousands of varieties of roses, with hundreds more being introduced to the market every year. Each with its own name. The official process of naming new breeds of flowers is complicated, expensive, and time consuming.

In addition to their registered names, some plants have also picked up quint names just because they grew close to someone creative. These vernacular names are, even though absolutely enchanting, not governed, and differ hugely from place to place (sometimes even within the same place!). In South Africa, people often refer to hydrangeas as Christmas roses. Here in Canada, a Christmas rose would more likely be a helleborus.

Which means we don't call all members of the rosa family, roses and it's highly unlikely that we will be able to identify every single rose variety even though we know it is a rose and we talk about "roses" that are not even closely related to the rosa family.

This is the main reason why Botanical Latin exists. Botanical Latin is a written language made up of bits of Latin and other languages so that we have a universal naming system and can understand which plants we are speaking of ... but (and I bet you knew there would be a *but*) we don't always agree on the pronunciation. It's entirely possible that a group of experts will point to the exact same flower and call it by a different sounding name.

So, my advice: say it as you say it. You really can't get it wrong if there is no right.

If the science part of floristry is interesting to you and adds to your creative process, by all means study the botanical plant names. If you need to order flowers, and talk about flowers in a way that someone needs to agree with which plant you are referring to, learn the Botanical Latin with the most popular (at least in your region) pronunciation. But if you find that this overwhelms you and gets in the way of your creative work, design with what you love and call it by the name that you know it by, or the name you use when you ask for it in the shop, or even better yet, what your grandmother used to call it.

There is a popular saying that goes like this:

Mispronouncing a Botanical Latin name for a plant is admirable because it means the person was interested enough to read it somewhere.

7715922

My dear Christine,

CPSIA information can be obtained
at www.ICGtesting.com
Printed in the USA
LVHW071914200219
608216LV00005B/5/P